PRIMARY MATHEMATICS 2A

HOME INSTRUCTOR GUIDE

Authored by: Jennifer Hoerst

Avyx

Primary Mathematics 2A
Copyright © 2003 by Jennifer Hoerst
Published by Avyx, Inc.
Reprinted 2012

Avyx, Inc.
8032 South Grant Way
Littleton, CO 80122-2705
USA

www.avyx.com
info@avyx.com
303-483-0140

ISBN 978-1-887840-78-1
Printed in the United States of America

Avyx, Inc., in an effort to help purchasers of the Singapore New Elementary Math 2A Textbook, is providing this Solutions Manual. Every effort has been made to eliminate errors. However, if you do find errors, we would also welcome your pointing these out to us. To give us feedback or to note error corrections, please sent an email to the author at jenny@singaporemath.com. As errors are detected and corrected, you may find the error corrections posted online at the author's web site, http://www.singaporemaths.com/errata/. If you have specific questions on the guides or want more help with the math, go to http://www.singaporemaths.com/forums/.

NOTE: This site is the sole property of Jennifer Hoerst and is not a site maintained by Avyx, Inc. This site is offered solely as a courtesy to help purchasers see corrections as Jennifer Hoerst posts them. All corrections captured will be included in updates to the manuals prior to their reprinting

Preface and General Instructions

This guide is meant to help instructors using *Primary Mathematics 2A* when teaching one student or a small group of students. It should be used as a guide and adapted as needed. It contains

 objectives,

 notes to the instructor, providing added explanation of concepts,

➤ instructional ideas and suggested activities,

 and ideas for games

to reinforce concepts from the

corresponding textbook pages, learning tasks, and

"homework" assignments.

Included is a <u>suggested</u> weekly schedule and pages for mental math (in the appendix). The schedule is simply to help you keep on track – you need to spend more time on a topic if necessary and less time if your student is proficient in the topic. Practices and reviews in the text are scheduled as they are encountered, and can be done independently by the student, or can be used as part of a lesson. Since some of the practice questions are challenging, they provide good opportunities for discussion. When there are several practices one after the other, you may want to go on to the next topic and insert the rest of the practices later to allow for more ongoing review. The mental math pages can be used as worksheets and many can also be done orally, with your student seeing the problem and answering out loud rather than writing the answer down. They can be used any time after they are referenced in this guide, and can be used more than once for more practice. So if four Mental Math pages are listed for one lesson, they are not meant to all be done during that lesson, but can be used any time after that lesson for review and mental math practice.

Answers to the workbook exercises are given at the end of this guide.

This guide can be used with both the third edition and the U.S. edition of *Primary Mathematics 2A*.

3d› indicates portions pertaining only to the third edition, and

US› indicates portions pertaining only to the US edition (except for number words).

U.S. spellings and conventions will be used in this guide. Answers involving number words will use the current U.S. convention of reserving the word "and" for the decimal and not using it in number words for whole numbers.

Contents

Answers to Mental Math

Appendix

Suggested Weekly Schedule

WB: Workbook   TB: Textbook

	Part	Lesson	Text pages	Exercises	Materials	Mental Math
	Unit 1 Numbers to 1000					
1	1 Looking Back	(1) Tens and Ones	6-8	WB Ex. 1	Place-value chart	Mental Math 1
		(2) Counting On and Counting Back	9	WB Ex. 2	Linking cubes or toothpicks Base-10 blocks Hundred chart	Mental Math 2 Mental Math 3
	2 Comparing Numbers	(3) Comparing Numbers within 100	10-11	WB Ex. 3	Hundred chart Index cards Base-10 blocks	
		(4) Practice	12	TB Practice 1A	Counters Number cubes	
	3 Hundreds, Tens and Ones	(5) Hundreds, Tens and Ones	13-16	WB Ex. 4	Place-value chart	
2		(6) 3-Digit Numbers	17-19	WB Ex. 5	Base-10 blocks toothpicks	
		(7) Writing and Comparing 3-digit Numbers	21	WB Ex. 6	Number discs Number cubes	
		(8) Counting On and Counting Back	20-21	WB Ex. 7		
	Unit 2 Addition and Subtraction					
	1 Meanings of Addition and Subtraction	(9) Part-Whole	22-24	WB Ex. 8	Counters Playing cards Base-10 blocks	Mental Math 4 Mental Math 5 Mental Math 6 Mental Math 7
		(10) Review mental math strategies				Mental Math 8 Mental Math 9 Mental Math 10
3		(11) Comparison by Subtraction	24	WB Ex. 9		
		(12) Word Problems	25-27	WB Ex. 10		
	2 Addition without Renaming	(13) Vertical Addition of 2-Digit Numbers	28-29	WB Ex. 11	Number discs Place-value chart	
		(14) Addition within 1000	29-30	WB Ex. 12	Base-10 blocks	
	3 Subtraction without Renaming	(15) Vertical Subtraction of 2-Digit Numbers	31-32	WB Ex. 13	Number discs Place-value chart	
4		(16) Subtraction within 1000	32-33	WB Ex. 14	Base-10 blocks	
		(17) Practice	34	TB Practice 2A	Playing cards	
		(18) Practice	35	TB Practice 2B		
	4 Addition with Renaming	(19) Renaming Ones in 2-Digit Addition	36-37	WB Ex. 15	Number discs Place-value chart	Mental Math 11
		(20) Renaming Ones in 3-Digit Addition	37-38	WB Ex. 16, #1	Playing cards Pennies, dimes Number cubes	Mental Math 12

	Part	Lesson	Text pages	Exercises	Materials	Mental Math
5		(21) Renaming Tens	38-39	WB Ex. 16, #2 WB Ex. 17		
		(22) Renaming Ones and Tens	39-40	WB Ex. 18		
		(23) Adding 3 Numbers	40	WB Ex. 19		
		(24 Practice	41	TB Practice 2C		
		(25) Practice	42	TB Practice 2D		
6	5 Subtraction with Renaming	(26) Renaming Tens in 2-Digit Subtraction	43-44	WB Ex. 20, #1	Number discs Place-value chart Playing cards Pennies, dimes Number cubes	Mental Math 13 Mental Math 14 Mental Math 15
		(27) Practice	48	TB Practice 2E		
		(28) Renaming Tens in 3-Digit Subtraction	44-45			Mental Math 16 Mental Math 17
		(29) Renaming Hundreds	45-46	WB Ex. 20 WB Ex. 21		
		(30) Renaming Tens and Hundreds	46-47	WB Ex. 22		
7		(31) Subtraction with No Tens	47	WB Ex. 23 WB Ex. 24		
		(32) Practice	49	TB Practice 2F		
		(33) Practice	50	TB Practice 2G		
		(34) Practice	51	TB Practice 2H		
	Review	(35)		WB Review 1		Mental Math 18 Mental Math 19 Mental Math 20 Mental Math 21 Mental Math 22
8	**Unit 3 Length**					
	1 Measuring Length in Meters	(36) Meters	52-53	WB Ex. 25	Meter stick	
		(37) Addition and Subtraction of Meters	54			
	2 Measuring Length in Centimeters	(38) Centimeters	55-56	WB Ex. 26	Ruler (cm) String Ruler Measuring Tape	
		(39) Curved Lines	57-58	WB Ex. 27		
		(40) Drawing Lines	58	**3d›** WB Ex. 28		
9	3 Measuring Length in Yards and Feet	(41) Yards and Feet	**US›**59-60		Yard stick Ruler	
	4 Measuring Length in Inches	(43) Inches	**US›**61-62	**US›** WB Ex. 28	Ruler	
		(43) Practice	**US›**63 **3d›**59	TB Practice 3A		
	Review	(44)		WB Review 2		
	Unit 4 Weight					
	1 Measuring Weight in Kilograms	(45) Kilograms	**US›**64-67 **3d›**60-63	WB Ex. 29	Balance Kilogram weight Scales	
10	2 Measuring Weight in Grams	(46) Grams	**US›**68-69 **3d›**64-65	WB Ex. 29	Balance Gram weight Scales	

	Part	Lesson	Text pages	Exercises	Materials	Mental Math
	3 Measuring Weight in Pound	(47) Pounds	US>70-71		Balance Pound weight Kilogram weight	
	4 Measuring Weight in Ounces	(48) Ounces, Practice	US>72-74 3d>66	TB Practice 4A	Balance or scales Ounce weight Gram weight	
	Review	(49) (50)	US>75 3d>67	TB Review A WB Review 3 WB Review 4		
11	**Unit 5 Multiplication and Division**					
	1 Multiplication	(51) Multiplication I	US>76-77 3d>68-69	WB Ex. 31	Cubes or counters Number cubes Graph paper	
		(52) Multiplication II	US>78 3d>70	WB Ex. 32 WB Ex. 33		
		(53) Arrays	US>78 3d>70	WB Ex. 34		
		(54)Practice	US>79 3d>71	TB Practice 5A		
	2 Division	(55) Sharing	US>80-82 3d>72-74	WB Ex. 35 WB Ex. 36	Cubes Counters	
12		(56) Grouping	US>83-84 3d>75-76	WB Ex. 37 WB Ex. 38		
		(57) Multiplication and Division Sentences	US>85 3d>77	WB Ex. 39		
		(58) Practice	US>86-87 3d>78-79	TB Practice 5B TB Practice 5C		
	Review	(59)		Review 5		
	Unit 6 Multiplication Tables of 2 and 3					
	1 Multiplication Table of 2	(60) Counting by Twos	US>88-90 3d>80-82	WB Ex. 40 WB Ex. 41	Multilink cubes Hundred chart Fact cards Playing cards Cubes or Counters	
13		(61) Multiplication Table of 2	US>90-91 3d>82-83	WB Ex. 42 WB Ex. 43		
		(62) Related Facts	US>91-92 3d>83-84	WB Ex. 44		
		(63) Multiplication F6acts for 2		WB Ex. 45		Mental Math 23 Mental Math 24 Mental Math 25
		(64) Word Problems, Practice	US>92-93 3d>84-85	WB Ex. 46		
	2 Multiplication Table of 3	(65) Counting by Threes	US>94-95 3d>86-87	WB Ex. 47 WB Ex. 48	Multilink cubes Hundred chart Counters Fact cards Playing cards Coin Playing cards	
14		(66) Related Facts	US>96 3d>88	WB Ex. 49		
		(67) Multiplication Table of 3	US>96-97 3d>88-89	WB Ex. 50 WB Ex. 51 WB Ex. 52		Mental Math 26 Mental Math 27 Mental Math 28
		(68) Multiplication Facts for 3	US>98 3d>90	WB Ex. 53		
		(69) Word Problems	US>97-98 3d>89-90	WB Ex. 54		
		(70) Practice	US>99 3d>91	WB Ex. 55 TB Practice 6C		

	Part	Lesson	Text pages	Exercises	Materials	Mental Math
15	3 Dividing by 2	(71) Division by 2	**US›** 100-101 **3d›**92-93	WB Ex. 56	Cubes or counters	Mental Math 29
		(72) Word Problems	**US›** 102-103 **3d›**94-95	WB Ex. 57		
		(73) Practice	**US›**104 **3d›**96	TB Practice 6D		
	4 Dividing by 3	(74) Division by 3	**US›**105 **3d›**97	WB Ex. 58	Playing cards Coin or die	
		(75) Division Facts for 2, Word Problems	**US›**106 **3d›**98	WB Ex. 59	Counters Division cards Multiplication	
16		(76) Practice	**US›**107 **3d›**99	TB Practice 6E WB Ex. 60	cards	Mental Math 30 Mental Math 31
		(77) Practice	**US›**108 **3d›**100	TB Practice 6F WB Ex. 61		Mental Math 32
	Review	(78-80)	**US›** 109-112 **3d›** 101-104	WB Review 6 WB Review 7 TB Review B TB Review C		

Additional Materials

Base-10 set. A set usually has 100 unit-cubes, 10 or more ten-rods, 10 hundred-flats, and 1 thousand-block,

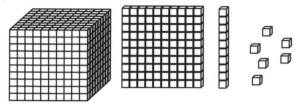

Place-value chart large enough to hold base-10 blocks. Draw it on a white-board as needed or on a sheets of paper taped together.

Hundreds	Tens	Ones

Number discs as an alternative to base-10 blocks. Use plastic or cardboard discs and write "1000" on a few, "100" on twenty discs, "10" on twenty discs, and "1" on twenty discs.

Multilink Cubes or Connect-a-Cubes. These are cubes, usually measuring about three-quarters of an inch or 2 cm, that can link to each other on all six sides.

Hundred chart

Make one or buy one with squares large enough to cover with counters or coins.

1	2	3	4	5	6	7	8	9	10
11	12	13	14	15	16	17	18	19	20
21	22	23	24	25	26	27	28	29	30
31	32	33	34	35	36	37	38	39	40
41	42	43	44	45	46	47	48	49	50
51	52	53	54	55	56	57	58	59	60
61	62	63	64	65	66	67	68	69	70
71	72	73	74	75	76	77	78	79	80
81	82	83	84	85	86	87	88	89	90
91	92	93	94	95	96	97	98	99	100

Counters (plastic discs) or **coins**.

Meter stick, **yard stick**, **ruler**, measuring tape in centimeters and inches. You can make a meter stick from cardboard and mark the centimeters.

Kitchen scale, if available.

Balance. A simple pan or bucket balance.

Number cubes: Dice or blank cubes that with labels.

Playing cards, index cards, number cubes for number cards and fact cards.

4 sets of number cards 0-10
Use two decks of **playing cards**. For one deck, remove the face cards and white out the 1 and the symbols on the tens card to make it into a 0. You can also white out the aces and draw a 1 in place of the A. Add in the tens from the other deck. Or just use the other deck without face cards for activities that involve numbers 1-10 only.

***Rainbow Rock* CD-ROM**
Optional computer CD-ROM with activities and games.

Unit 1 – Numbers to 1000

Part 1 - Looking Back

(1) Tens and Ones (pp. 6-8)

- ➢ Count within 100 by grouping by tens.
- ➢ Read and write 2-digit numbers and corresponding number words.
- ➢ Relate 2-digit numbers to tens and ones.

In *Primary Mathematics 1*, students learned to relate 2-digit numbers to the place value concept. This place-value concept is reviewed and reinforced in this section. All the following activities may not be necessary, since this is a review.

You may wish to use the Mental Math worksheets 1, 2 and 3 in the appendix to start reviewing addition and subtraction facts.

➤ Use a **place-value chart** and objects such as **toothpicks, connect-a-cubes, or craft sticks** that can be grouped or bundled into tens. Give your student a number of objects (e.g., 34). Ask for suggestions on how to count the objects. He should count them by grouping them into tens and placing them on the place value chart. Show how the number can be represented on a place-value chart with numerals, as a number bond for tens and ones, written as 3 tens 4 ones, and finally as 34. Point to the 4 in the number and ask your student for the number's place (ones place) and value (4). The number written farthest to the right, or the number usually written last, tells us how many ones there are. Then point to the 3 and ask for the place (tens) and value (30). A number written one place to the left of the ones tells us how many tens there are. By their place in the number, we know whether it is a ten or a one.

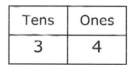

Tens	Ones
3	4

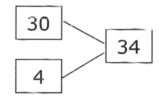

3 tens 4 ones

34

Ask questions such as:

30 and 4 make _____	(34)
34 is 30 and _____	(4)
34 is 4 more than _____	(30)
30 is 4 less than _____	(34)
34 is 3 tens and _____ ones	(4)
34 is 2 tens and _____ ones	(14)
34 is _____ ten and 24 ones	(1)

Have your student practice writing number words. Dictate some number words. Start with single words; e.g. two, three, four, five, six, seven, eight, nine, ten, twenty, thirty, forty, fifty, sixty, seventy, eighty, ninety, one hundred
Then do words in combination; forty-one, fifty-seven .... Point out that there is a hyphen between the tens and the ones.

Have your student practice counting by tens, both forwards and backwards.

p. 6
Learning Tasks 1-3, pp. 7-8
For learning task 2, also have your student count backwards by tens.

1. (a) **45**   (b) **45**   (c) **45**   (d) **45**
2. **100** stamps
3. (a) **26**   (b) **43**   (c) **5** tens **7** ones = **57**

Workbook Exercise 1

(2) Counting On and Counting Back (p. 9)

➢ Count on 1, 2, 10, and 20 to a number less than 100.
➢ Count back 1, 2, 10, or 20 from a number less than 100.
➢ Practice math facts.

➤ Use a **hundred chart**
Discuss the order of numbers on the chart:
o   Each number is one less than the number to the right of it.
o   Each number is one more than the number to the left of it.
o   Each number is ten more than the number above it.
o   Each number is ten less than the number below it.
Point to a number and ask your student to count backward or forward from it
by 1, 2, 10, or 20.

Circle two numbers at random on the chart and ask your student to count
forward or backward, first by tens and then by ones from one number to the
other.

Write down a 2-digit number and/or show the number using base-10 blocks
and a place-value chart. Ask your student to count on or back from it by 1, 2,
10, or 20. Point out which digit she is adding to or subtracting from in terms of
tens or ones. For example, in 64 + 20 she is adding 2 *tens*. So she adds it to
the 6 *tens*. Include numbers that "go around the corner" or involve changing to
the next higher or lower ten, e.g. 29 + 2 or 31 – 2.

Learning Tasks 4-6, p. 9
These problems should not be rewritten vertically. Your student should be able
to determine whether to add to or subtract from the tens or the ones. If your
student has problems with these exercises, illustrate with **base-10 blocks** as
you go through the learning tasks with her.

4. (a) 66	(b) 64	(c) 75	(d) 55
5. (a) 67	(b) 63	(c) 85	(d) 45
6. (a) 81	(b) 82	(c) 90	(d) 100
(e) 79	(f) 78	(g) 70	(h) 60

Workbook Exercise 2

Part 2 – Comparing Numbers

(3) Comparing Numbers within 100 (pp. 10-11)

➢ Compare and order numbers within 100 (review).
➢ Recognize and use the symbols > for "is greater than" and < for "is less than".

In *Primary Mathematics 1*, students learned to compare and order numbers within 100. Here, the symbols for greater than ">" and less than "<" are introduced.

By part 2 of Unit 2, students should be able to easily recall the math facts for addition and subtraction through 20. Spend some time each day, about 5 minutes at a time, if necessary, reviewing addition and subtraction through 20. Use drill sheets, computer games, card games, flash cards, or whatever your student learns the best with.

➤ Write down two to five numbers within 100, e.g., 43, 54, 19, 34 on **index cards** or separate pieces of paper. Ask your student to arrange them in order. He must first look at the tens, then the ones to determine their order. Use **base-10 blocks** or discs to illustrate, if necessary. Lead your student to see that the order is determined by the digit in the tens place. If that digit is the same for the numbers being compared, then the digit in the ones place is used to order the numbers.

p. 10
The open end of the symbols < and > is facing the greater amount. To help the student to remember this, he can associate the symbols with the mouth of a greedy crocodile who always wants to eat the "bigger" or greater number.

Learning tasks 1-3, p. 11

1. (a) **>**   (b) **<**
   (c) **>**   (d) **<**   (e) **<**   (f) **>**

2. (a) **39**   (b) **30**   (c) **56**   (d) **98**

3. **50, 59, 90, 95**

 Workbook Exercise 3

(4) Practice 1A (p. 12)

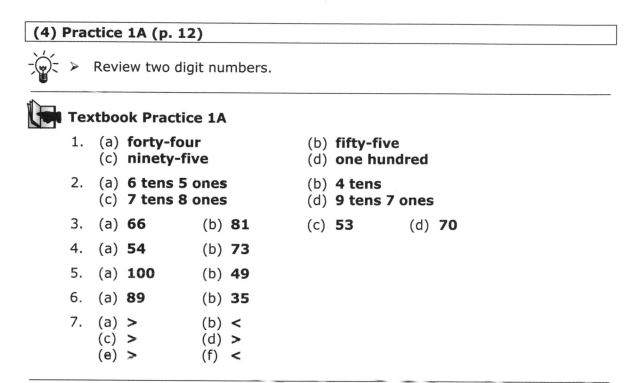

💡 ➢ Review two digit numbers.

📖 **Textbook Practice 1A**

1. (a) **forty-four**   (b) **fifty-five**
   (c) **ninety-five**   (d) **one hundred**

2. (a) **6 tens 5 ones**   (b) **4 tens**
   (c) **7 tens 8 ones**   (d) **9 tens 7 ones**

3. (a) **66**   (b) **81**   (c) **53**   (d) **70**

4. (a) **54**   (b) **73**

5. (a) **100**   (b) **49**

6. (a) **89**   (b) **35**

7. (a) **>**   (b) **<**
   (c) **>**   (d) **>**
   (e) **>**   (f) **<**

🎲 **Arrow Game**

Material: **Hundred chart**, **counters**, paper, pencil

Arrows represent movements on the grid.

12 → =13   12 ← =11   12 ↑ = 2   12 ↓ = 22
12 ↘ = 23   12 ↙ = 21   12 ↖ = 1   12 ↗ = 3

Give arrow problems, such as:

63 ↑ ↓ → → = ?   (answer = 65)
27 ↗ → → ↓ ← ↓ ↙ = ?   (answer = 48)
? → → → ↙ = 64   (answer = 52)

Let your student write arrow directions between two numbers and see if you can follow his directions.

🎲 **Roll the Tens**

Material: **Number cube (1-6)**

Each player draws two lines on their paper for tens and ones.   ___ ___
Each player throws the number cubes once, then decides whether the number thrown should be a ten or a one and writes it on the appropriate line. Then each player throws the number cube a second time and writes the number on the remaining line. The player with the highest 2-digit number gets a point. Play continues until one player gets 10 points.

Part 3 – Hundreds, Tens, and Ones

(5) Hundreds, Tens, and Ones (pp. 13-16)

➢ Relate 3-digit numbers to hundreds, tens, and ones.
➢ Read and write 3-digit numbers.

The concept of place value is extended to hundreds in this section. Students should have a good knowledge of place value for addition and subtraction with renaming, which will be introduced in the next unit.

➤ Use a **place-value chart** and **base-10 blocks**. Have your student count as she places ones in the ones column. Write the number below the ones column. When she gets to 9, ask what we should do now to be able to write a number with one more. To add another one, we make a group of 10 and move it to the tens place to show that we have a ten. Trade the 9 ones plus one more one for a ten and place that in the tens column. Write 1 under the tens column and the 0 under the ones column. Explain that the "1" is one place over, in the place for tens, and shows that we have one ten. The "0" shows that we have no ones. Ask your student to add more tens to the tens place and count as you write the numbers. When she gets to 90, ask how we can show one more ten. We put the tens into groups of ten and move them over one more place. Ask her if she knows what the new place is called. It is the hundreds place. Have her trade the 9 tens plus one more for a hundred-flat and place that in the hundreds column. Write the number 100, with the digits under the appropriate columns.

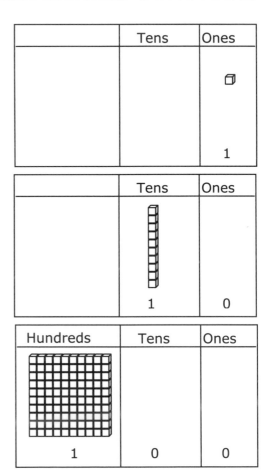

Now the 1 is in the third place from the left, and tells us that we have 1 hundred. The 0's tell us that there are no tens or ones. She can then continue adding hundreds to the chart until she has 9 hundreds. The next hundred needs a new place for ten hundreds, called the thousands place.

➤ Do an activity similar to that shown on p. 13. Give your student some **toothpicks**, straws, or beads. Have him determine how many items there are by grouping first into tens, and then into hundreds. Then have him place the bundles on a **place-value chart** and write the number. This is a time-consuming activity. If your student has a good understanding of place value he may not have the patience for this activity. Do the next one instead, but you can give him too many ones or tens so that he has to group some of them.

Use a **place-value chart** and **base-10 blocks.** Give your student some hundreds, tens, and ones. Have him place them on the place value chart, say the number, and write the number. Rewrite the number in terms of hundreds, tens and ones. For example,

    482 = 4 hundreds, 8 tens, 2 ones = 400 + 80 + 2
    203 = 2 hundreds, 0 tens, 3 ones = 200 + 3

Ask questions such as the following, illustrating with **base-10 blocks** if necessary:

    How much is 10 ones?   (10)
    How much is 10 tens?   (100)
    How much is 100 tens? (1000)
    How much is 80 tens?   (800)
    How much is 21 tens?   (210)

➤ Draw the following chart.

1	2	3	4	5
6	7	8	9	10
11	12	13	14	15
16	17	18	19	20

Ask her if she sees any pattern. The purpose of this problems is to focus on the place of each digit. She should notice that the number in the ones place alternates. For example, in the first column the pattern for the ones is 1, 6, 1, 6, ... Give her some three digit numbers, such as 345, 952, 169, or 243. Ask which column the number would belong in if the table were extended.

Pages 13-14
Learning Tasks 1-3, pp. 15-16

1. (a) **346**   (b) **4 hundreds 3 tens 7 ones = 437**

3. (a) **258**   (b) **470**   (c) **809**

 Workbook Exercise 4

(6) 3-Digit Numbers (pp. 17-19)

- ➢ Relate hundreds, tens, and ones to currency bills.
- ➢ Rename currency bills
- ➢ Relate 3-digit numbers to number discs
- ➢ Rename number discs.

Number discs are a useful alternative to base-10 blocks, since they represent a more abstract representation of place value. The student must understand that there are 10 ones in a disc labeled as 10, rather than seeing 10 ones put together to form a rod as with base-10 blocks. The text makes extensive use of number discs to illustrate concepts involving base 10. They can be easily drawn on a white board or paper. You can label counters as number discs for use in this and succeeding lessons. Write 1 on the front of 20 discs, 10 on the front of 20 discs, 100 on the front of 20 discs, and 1000 on the front of some discs (1000-discs will be used more in *Primary Mathematics 3*) with a permanent marker. The reverse sides can be used as regular counters.

Learning Tasks 4-5, pp. 17-18
Remind your student that a $10 bill has the same value as ten $1 bills. A $100 bill has the same value as ten $10 bills.

4.   (c) **10**   5.   **10**

> Show your student the **number discs**. Lead your student to realize that the 10 on the 10-disc means that the disc stands for 10 things, and so it has the same value as ten 1-discs. Similarly, a 100-disc represents 100 things, and has the same value as ten 10-discs. A 1000-disc has the same value as ten 100-discs.

Use the number discs and a **place-value chart** and ask the following questions, illustrating with number discs:

o How many 1's are in 10 tens?	100
o How many 1's are in 10 hundreds?	1000
o How many 1's are in 21 tens?	210
o How many 10's are in 210 1's?	21
o How many 10's are in 200 1's?	20
o How many 100's are in 200 1's?	2
o How many 100's are in 20 10's?	2

➤ Use the **number discs** and a **place-value chart**. Place a number a few ones less than a multiple of a hundred on the place-value chart. Ask your student to count up by adding ones to the chart, and trading in ten 1-discs for a 10-disc or ten 10-discs for a 100-disc. For example, put 498 on the chart. Say and write "498." Your student adds a one, says "four hundred ninety-nine," and you write "499." He gets another one, but can't put it on the chart since the ones column can only hold nine. So he must group it with the nine already there, and trade it in for a 10-disc. But the tens column already has nine tens, so he must group the ten with the other nine tens and trade it in for a 100-disc and place that on the chart in the hundreds column. He says "five hundred" and you write "500." Similarly, place a number a few units above a multiple of a hundred and have the student count down by removing ones from the chart, trading in a 100 disc for ten 10-discs or a 10-disc for ten 1-discs. For example, put 201 on the chart. He must trade in a 100-disc for ten 10-discs, and then a 10-disc for ten 1-discs to go from 200 to 199.

Learning Tasks 6-8, pp. 18-19.

6. (a) **100**   (b) **1000**
7. **6, 2, 3**
8. (a) **467**   (b) **250**   (c) **306**

Workbook Exercise 5

(7) Writing and Comparing 3-Digit Numbers (p. 21)

> ➤ Write number words for 3-digit numbers.
> ➤ Compare and order 3-digit numbers.

In the 3rd edition of *Primary Mathematics*, the word "and" is used in number words. In the U.S., the current convention is to reserve the word "and" for the decimal point when naming decimals as fractions, e.g. 132.3 is "one hundred thirty two and three tenths".

This guide will use the U.S. convention for number words. If you prefer using the convention in the 3d edition, add the word "and" after the word hundred in the answers to exercises asking the student to write a number in words.

➤ Make sure your student can spell the number words.

one	eleven	ten	hundred
two	twelve	twenty	
three	thirteen	thirty	
four	fourteen	forty	
five	fifteen	fifty	
six	sixteen	sixty	
seven	seventeen	seventy	
eight	eighteen	eighty	
nine	nineteen	ninety	

Use three **number cubes**. Label one with the numbers 9, 8, 7, 6, 5, 4, the second with the numbers 1, 2, 3, 4, 5, 6, and the third the third number cubes with numbers your student has the most trouble spelling. Throw all three number cubes. Have your student form a 3-digit number and then write the number in numerals and in words.

Ask your student how many three digit numbers can be made from the digits 1, 2, and 3, using each digit only once. (6 numbers: 123, 132, 213, 231, 312, 321) Help her develop a systematic way of listing the numbers; for example, start with all possibilities that begin with 1.

Write the six numbers one above the other, with the digits aligned. Compare the numbers, discussing which is greatest, or which is smallest, and why. Point out that when we compare numbers, we first compare the values in the largest place, in this case, hundreds. If they are equal, we then compare the values in the tens place. If those are equal, we compare the values in the ones place. Use two of the numbers and write their comparison using the symbols ">" or "<", e.g.: 312 < 321.

> Give your student some additional numbers to compare or order. Illustrate with number discs if necessary. Include comparison of a 2-digit number to a 3-digit number, e.g. 31 and 123. Though the first digit of the second number is smaller than the first digit of the first number, the actual number is larger, since the first digit is in the hundreds place. You can show this by using 0 as a place holder to show that there are no hundreds (031).

 Practice 1B, #1-5, p. 21
Do these problems with your student as part of this lesson.

1. (a) **three hundred thirty**   (b) **one hundred forty-four**
   (c) **two hundred fifty-five**   (d) **six hundred eight**

2. (a) **6 hundreds 4 tens 5 ones**   (b) **7 hundreds 2 tens**
   (c) **4 hundreds 9 ones**   (d) **9 hundreds**

3. (a) **704**   (b) **540**   (c) **304**   (d) **820**

4. (a) **>**   (b) **<**   (c) **>**   (d) **>**

5. (a) **99, 410, 609**   (b) **104, 140, 401, 410**

 Roll the Hundreds

Materials: **Number cubes**, paper and pencil for each player.

Procedure: Write three dashes on the paper for each place value. Each player takes turns rolling a number cube. After each roll, the player must decide whether to write the number in the hundreds place, the tens place, or the ones place. Once written, it must remain in that place. The highest number wins after all players have had a turn. The number cube is rolled three times, once for each dash. For example, you go first and throw a 5. You decide to write it in the tens place: ___ _5_ __. You then throw a 3. You write it in the ones place. On the next roll you get a 2. Oops. It has to go in the hundreds place. Your number is _2_ _5_ _3_. Well, you still have a chance, if the other player ends up with 1 in the hundreds place.

Workbook Exercise 6

(8) Counting On and Counting Back (pp. 20-21)

> ➢ Count up by 1's, 10's, or 100's.
> ➢ Count back by 1's, 10's, or 100's.

➤ Use a **place-value chart** and **number discs** or **base-10 blocks**. Place a 3-digit number on the place-value chart and write the number. Ask the student to give the number that is 1 more or less, 10 more or less, or 100 more or less than the number on the chart. Be sure to include numbers where the ones or tens have to be regrouped. For example:
- o   What number is 1 less than 200?   (199)
- o   What number is 10 more than 495? (505)
- o   What number is 100 less than 640? (540)

Learning Tasks 9-10, p. 20

9. (a) **254**   (b) **133**   (c) **241**
10. (a) **800**   (b) **490**   (c) **570**

Practice 1B, #6-8, p. 21

6. (a) **300**   (b) **779**
7. (a) **472**   (b) **790**
8. (a) **699**   (b) **505**

➤ Give your student a 3-digit number. Have him count forwards to 1000 and backwards to one by tens. For example: 569, 579, 589, 599, 609 ...

Give your student two 3-digit numbers. Have her count from one number to the other, both forwards and backwards, first by hundreds, then by tens, then by ones. For example, if the two numbers are 248 and 572:

Forward: 248, 348, 448, 548, 558, 568, 569, 570, 571, 572
Backward: 572, 472, 372, 272, 262, 252, 251, 250, 249, 248

➤ Write some patterns for your student. The ones, tens, or hundreds should increase or decrease by 1 or 2. Try some where the digits in two places increase or decrease, or where they increase in one place value and decrease in the other. Your student should complete the number pattern by determining which place value changes. For example:

        123, 143, 163, _____
        932, 832, 732, _____
        791, 782, 773, 764, _____

 Workbook Exercise 7

Unit 2 – Addition and Subtraction

Part 1 – Meanings of Addition and Subtraction

(9) Part-Whole (pp. 22-24)

➢ Review the part-whole concept of addition and subtraction.
➢ Use addition to find a whole and subtraction to find a part.
➢ Write four related addition and subtraction sentences for a given situation within 20.

In *Primary Mathematics 1*, addition and subtraction were associated with the part-whole concept of number bonds.

To find the whole when given two parts, add.

$5 + 3 = ?$

To find a missing part when given the whole and one part, subtract.

$8 - 5 = ?$

This part-whole concept can also be modeled as follows:

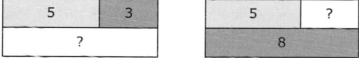

It can be tricky for younger children to model problems by themselves until they have a better feel for numbers and can determine reasonable proportions for the bars. However, you can use modeling to illustrate the problem for your student. Modeling will be developed more fully in *Primary Mathematics 3*. In this guide, simple models will used in the solutions for some of the problems, to be used at your discretion.

In *Primary Mathematics 1*, the students also learned that with any number bond they can write a family of two addition and two subtraction facts. This will also be reviewed in this section.

$$5 + 3 = 8 \qquad 8 - 5 = 3$$
$$3 + 5 = 8 \qquad 8 - 3 = 5$$

➤ Use some uniform-sized **objects**, such as multilink cubes, coins, counters, or buttons. Line some up to show two parts, and underneath line some up to show the whole. Cover up or remove the whole or one of the parts. Ask the student to supply the missing whole or part. Write the corresponding equations. Uncover the missing whole or part.

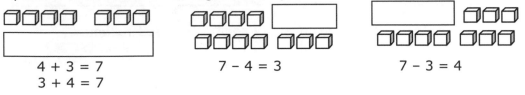

$4 + 3 = 7$ $7 - 4 = 3$ $7 - 3 = 4$
$3 + 4 = 7$

---

 p. 22

Point out that there are two parts, the number of cars Ali has and the number of cars David has. We want to find the whole, the number of cars they have altogether. We add the two parts together.

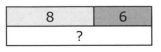

$8 + 6 = $ **14**   They have **14** toy cars altogether.

Learning task 1, p. 23

Point out that we are given the whole, the number of cars Ali and David have altogether, and one part, the number of cars Ali has. To find the other part, the number of cars David has, we subtract the known part from the whole.

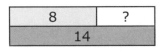   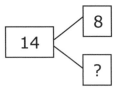

$14 - 8 = $ **6**   David has **6** toy cars.

Learning task 2, 23

Write the number bond and show how we can write four number facts from the number bond.

$7 + 5 = $ **12** $5 + 7 = $ **12**
$12 - 5 = $ **7** $12 - 7 = $ **5**

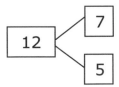

Learning task 3, p. 24

$9 + 3 = $ **12** $3 + 9 = $ **12**
$12 - 3 = $ **9** $12 - 9 = $ **3**

➤ If necessary, review addition and subtraction of 1-digit numbers and tens. You can use the following games, and/or the Mental Math worksheets 4-7 in the appendix. You can use the mental math pages in a variety of ways. For example, you can have your student do one page several times a week. You can have her do one column daily. You can time her and use the same sheet several times to see if she can improve her time.

If your student did not use *Primary Mathematics 1*, you may want to use base-10 blocks to illustrate "making a ten" in addition or "subtracting from a ten" in subtraction, particularly if your student knows his facts through 10 but not through 20 yet.

Pyramid (fact practice)

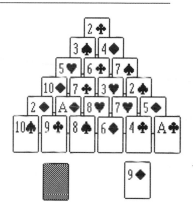

Material: Deck of **playing cards**, without picture cards (Joker, King, Queen, Jack)

Procedure: Set the cards up in a pyramid of 6 rows of overlapping cards as shown. Pick a target number from 6 to 16. The goal is to remove as many cards as possible. The cards must be fully exposed to be removed, and must add up to the target number. If none can be combined to make the target number, turn over the top card of the face-down pile. If no match can be made, put it face up in a discard pile. The top card of the discard pile can be used at any time, but no others in that pile. The game ends when all the cards in the face-down pile have been turned over. The goal is to get rid of as much of the pyramid as possible.

War

Material: Playing cards without picture cards. Aces are ones.

Procedure: Deal out all cards. Cards are kept face down.
Game 1: Each player turns over 2 cards and adds them. The player with the highest total gets all the cards that have been turned over or a point. If the total is the same then the player with the highest card wins the point.
Game 2: Each player turns over 2 cards and adds 10 to the number on the first card to get a number between 10 and 20. The player then subtracts the value on the second card from this number. The student with the smallest answer gets all the cards that have been turned over. If the answer is the same for both players, the player with the smallest card wins the point.
The player with the most cards after all cards have been turned over or the most points wins.

 **Workbook Exercise 8**

(10) Review mental math

 ➤ Review mental math strategies.

In Primary Mathematics 1, students also learned various strategies for adding and subtracting without the formal algorithm.

- Add 1, 2, or 3 by counting on.
  59 + 2 = 61; count on 60, 61.

- Subtract 1, 2, or 3 by counting back.
  51 – 2 = 49; count back 50, 49.

- Add two 1-digit numbers whose sum is greater than 10 by making a 10. (This strategy is particularly useful for students who know the addition and subtraction facts through 10, but have trouble memorizing the addition and subtraction facts through 20.)

  7 + 5 = 12

  $$7 + 5 = 10 + 2 = 12$$
  $$\overset{\diagup\diagdown}{3 \quad 2}$$

  $$7 + 5 = 2 + 10 = 12$$
  $$\overset{\diagup\diagdown}{2 \quad 5}$$

- Add tens to 2 digit numbers by adding the tens.

  48 + 20 = 68

  $$48 + 20 = 68$$
  $$\overset{\diagup\diagdown}{8 \quad 40}$$

- Subtract tens from a 2-digit numbers by subtracting the tens.

  48 – 20 = 28

  $$48 - 20 = 20 + 8 = 28$$
  $$\overset{\diagup\diagdown}{8 \quad 40}$$

- Add a 1-digit number to a 2-digit number by adding the ones together.

  47 + 2 = 49

  $$47 + 2 = 40 + 9 = 49$$
  $$\overset{\diagup\diagdown}{40 \quad 7}$$

- Add a 1-digit number to a 2-digit number where adding the ones results in a number greater than 10
  o by making a 10, or
  o by using basic addition facts.

  68 + 5 = 73

  $$68 + 5 = 70 + 3 = 73$$
  $$\overset{\diagup\diagdown}{2 \quad 3}$$

- Subtract a 1-digit number from a 2-digit number when there are enough ones by subtracting the ones.

  47 – 2 = 45

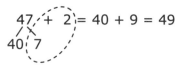

  $$68 + 5 = 60 + 13 = 73$$
  $$\overset{\diagup\diagdown}{60 \quad 8}$$
  $$47 - 2 = 45$$
  $$\overset{\diagup\diagdown}{40 \quad 7}$$

- Subtract a 1-digit number from a 2-digit number when there are not enough ones
  - by subtracting from a 10, or
  - by using basic subtraction facts.

65 – 8 = 57

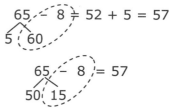

➤ You may want to review addition and subtraction within 100. Use **base-10 blocks** to illustrate. Write the problems in terms of tens and ones. You can use Mental Math worksheets 8-10 for additional practice.

45 + 3 = 48
4 tens 5 ones + 3 ones = 4 tens 8 ones

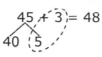

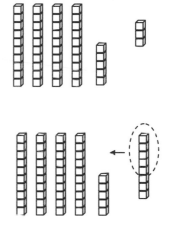

45 + 8 = 53
Make tens
4 tens 5 ones + 8 ones
= 4 tens 5 ones + 5 ones + 3 ones
= 5 tens 3 ones

Or use addition facts
4 tens 5 ones + 8 ones = 4 tens + 13 ones
                       = 4 tens + 1 ten 3 ones
                       = 5 tens 3 ones

45 – 3 = 42
4 tens 5 ones – 3 ones = 4 tens 2 ones

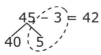

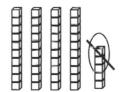

40 – 8 = 42
4 tens – 8 ones = 3 tens 2 ones

40 – 8 = 32

45 − 8 = 37
Subtract from a ten
4 tens 5 ones − 8 ones = 4 tens − 8 ones + 5 ones
                      = 3 tens 2 ones + 5 ones
                      = 3 tens 7 ones

45 − 8 = 37
5   40

Or use subtraction facts
4 tens 5 ones − 8 ones = 3 tens 15 ones − 8 ones
                      = 3 tens 7 ones

50 + 40 = 90
5 tens + 4 tens = 9 tens

50 − 40 = 10
5 tens − 4 tens = 1 ten

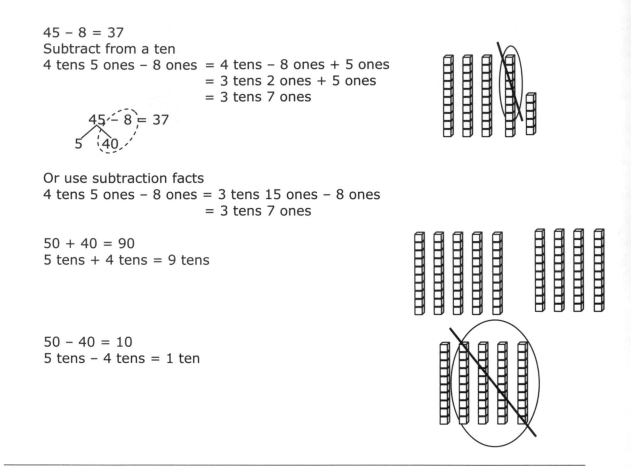

War

Material: **Playing cards** without picture cards. Aces are ones.

Procedure: Deal out all cards. Cards are kept face down. Each player turns over three cards. The first two cards are the tens and ones of a 2-digit number. The third card is the ones of a 1-digit number.

Game 1: Each player adds their 2-digit and 1-digit numbers. The one with the highest total gets all the cards or a point.

Game 2: Each player subtracts their 1-digit number from the 2-digit number. The player with the lowest answer gets all the cards that have been turned over or a point.

The player with the most cards after all cards have been turned over or the most points wins.

---

(11) Comparison by Subtraction (p. 24)

> ➢ Compare sets by subtraction.
> ➢ Relate "more than" and "less than" to addition and subtraction.
> ➢ Write four related addition and subtraction sentences for a given situation within 100.

In *Primary Mathematics 1*, the student learned that subtraction can be used when comparing two sets of objects to find out how many more or how many fewer objects are in one set than in the other set.
For example, there are 10 ice cream cones and 6 ice cream bars.

To find out how many more ice cream cones there are than ice cream bars, we subtract: 10 - 6 = 4

There are 4 more ice cream cones than ice cream bars (or 4 fewer ice cream bars than ice cream cones).

This can be modeled:

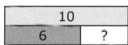

If necessary, use **objects** to illustrate this concept. Line up the objects and ask for the difference. Show that the difference is found by subtraction.

 Display two sets of objects in two lines, such as yellow and red counters.

10 – 6 = 4

Ask students which set has more objects. How many more? Which has less? How many less? Show that we can find how many more or less there are in one set than the other by subtraction.

Use different ways of expressing the difference between the two sets:
6 is 4 less than 10
10 is 4 more than 6
4 less than 10 is 6
4 more than 6 is 10

Learning Task 4, p. 24

Have your student count the number of bananas in each set.

Set A has 5 bananas, Set B has 9 bananas.

Remind him that he can find out how many more bananas there are in Set B than in Set A by subtracting: 9 - 5 = 4

Also say: 9 is 4 more than 5.
            4 is 5 less than 9.
            The difference between 9 and 5 is 4.

(a)   There are **4** more bananas in Set B than in Set A.

(b)   9 - 5 = **4**

Learning **Task 5, p. 24**

Two numbers, 14 and 8, are being compared by subtraction.

(a)   14 - 8 = **6**

(b)   8 less than 14 is **6**.

Also say: 14 is 6 more than 8.
            8 is 6 less than 14
            The difference between 14 and 8 is 6.

Workbook Exercise 9

(12) Word Problems (pp. 25-27)

➢ Review addition and subtraction of 2-digit numbers (no renaming).
➢ Apply part-whole and comparison by subtraction concepts to 2-digit numbers.
➢ Solve word problems involving mental addition and subtraction within 100.

In Primary Mathematics 1, students learned to mentally add and subtract 2-digit numbers.

- Add a 2-digit number to a 2-digit number by adding first the tens and then the ones.

  43 + 25 = 68

$$43 \xrightarrow{+\ 20} 63 \xrightarrow{+\ 5} 68$$

- Subtract a 2-digit number from a 2-digit number by subtracting first the tens and then the ones.

$$75 \xrightarrow{-\ 30} 45 \xrightarrow{-\ 1} 44$$

  75 – 31 = 44

Problems involving addition and subtraction of 2-digit numbers will not involve renaming in this part of the unit (e.g., 42 – 18 or 46 + 17).

➤ If necessary, use **base-10 blocks** or other base-10 material to review addition and subtraction of 2-digit numbers. You do not need to include problems that involve renaming at this point (e.g. 42 – 7).

43 + 25 = 68
4 tens + 2 tens = 6 tens,
3 ones + 5 ones = 8 ones,
4 tens 3 ones + 2 tens 5 ones
                = 6 tens 8 ones

You can illustrate addition of 2-digit numbers with number bonds:

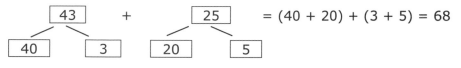

$$= (40 + 20) + (3 + 5) = 68$$

47 - 4 = 43
4 tens 7 ones - 4 ones = 4 tens 3 ones

47 - 24 = 23
4 tens - 2 tens = 2 tens,
7 ones - 4 ones = 3 ones,
4 tens 7 ones - 2 tens 4 ones = 2 tens 3 ones

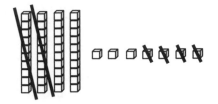

You can illustrate subtraction of 2-digit numbers
with number bonds:

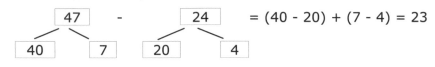

= (40 - 20) + (7 - 4) = 23

 Learning Tasks 6-8, p. 25

6. **56**

7. **14**

8. **45   32**
    45   13

Learning Tasks 9-12, pp 26-27
When doing word problems, ask questions such as: Are we given the total
amount of something? Do we have two parts or a part and a whole (the total)?
How do we find the total? How do we find the other part? If two amounts are
being compared, how do we find how much more one is than the other? Which
amount do we subtract?

9.   34 + 5 = **39**

10. 24 + 32 = **56**

11. 78 – 40 = **38**

12. 48 - 32 = **16**

     This is a comparison.

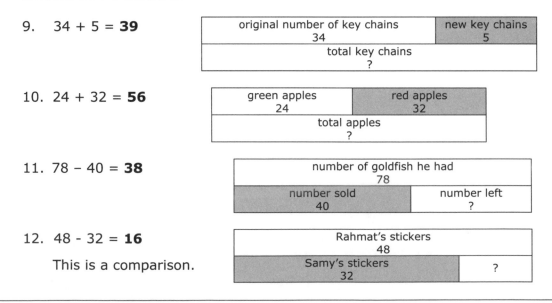

 Workbook Exercise 10

Part 2 – Addition without Renaming

Up to this point, the student has been adding and subtracting 2-digit numbers in a horizontal format using a variety of techniques. In this and the next section, the formal algorithm for addition and subtraction is introduced, where the problem is worked in a vertical format starting with addition or subtraction of the ones in the ones place, followed by addition or subtraction of the tens in the tens place, then addition and subtraction of the hundreds in the hundreds place, as illustrated on pages 28 and 31.

Students are first introduced to vertical addition with numbers within 100. If your student is proficient at adding these horizontally, he may find this section tedious. You can tell him he will be using this method with larger numbers and he should concentrate on having him line up the digits correctly for the learning tasks. It is not necessary for him to rewrite the problems in exercise 11 vertically unless he is having trouble lining up the digits, in which case, have him rewrite a few of them for practice.

Your student should have a good knowledge of place value and the basic addition facts within 20. If these facts are not yet mastered, provide opportunities to practice and master them.

As your student becomes more proficient with adding and subtracting 3-digit numbers using the vertical format, including situations involving renaming, she may be able to solve the problems in a horizontal format, particularly if she has a good sense of place value and can align the digits mentally. She may also use an alternative algorithm or strategy where the numbers in the highest place value are added first, using mental math techniques. Do not discourage her from developing her own methods. Flexibility with numbers indicates a good understanding of place value. Do make sure she understands the formal algorithm, though, since it is a useful algorithm for all types of problems. Your student should develop a feeling for when she can get a correct answer adding mentally, and when it is better to use the formal algorithms. Which method she uses can change with practice, and also be different under different circumstances.

(13) Vertical Addition of 2-Digit Numbers (pp. 28-29)

➤ Add ones, tens, or hundreds.
➤ Add within 100, without renaming, using the formal algorithm for addition.

Learning Task 1, p. 29

Ask your student to solve these problems mentally. After he gives the answers, show these problems rewritten vertically. Then write the problem where the ones, tens, and hundreds are combined. Ones are added to ones, tens to tens, and hundreds to hundreds.

1. (a) **5**   (b) **50**   (c) **500**

$$
\begin{array}{r} 2 \\ +\ 3 \\ \hline 5 \end{array}
\qquad
\begin{array}{r} 2\,0 \\ +\ 3\,0 \\ \hline 5\,0 \end{array}
\qquad
\begin{array}{r} 2\,0\,0 \\ +3\,0\,0 \\ \hline 5\,0\,0 \end{array}
\qquad
\begin{array}{r} 2\,2\,2 \\ +3\,3\,3 \\ \hline 5\,5\,5 \end{array}
$$

Tell your student that she will learn a new way for adding numbers that she will use for larger numbers that are not easy to add mentally. Since there are more place values to keep track of, we can write one number on top of the other, lining up the digits in each place.

Use **number discs** and a **place-value chart**. Write an addition equation for 2-digit numbers in vertical format. The sum of the digits in each place should be less than 10.

Show your student that when we write the numbers one below the other, we line up the ones with the ones, and the tens with the tens, just as we do in the columns on a place-value chart. You can draw a dotted line to separate the columns of digits. Tell your student that we can add the ones first, and then the tens.

Say "4 ones plus 3 ones equal 7 ones" and write the 7 under the ones. Point out that you are writing the total number of ones in the ones place, which is under the other ones. Say "2 tens plus 4 tens is 6 tens" and write 6 in the tens place. You can emphasize that the tens is written in the tens place by writing the tens and ones separately, and then writing their sum.

Hundreds	Tens	Ones
	⑩ ⑩	① ① / ① ①
	⑩ ⑩ / ⑩ ⑩	① ① / ①

$$
\begin{array}{r} 2\,|\,4 \\ +\ 4\,|\,3 \\ \hline 6\,|\,7 \end{array}
\qquad
\begin{array}{r} 2\ 4 \\ +\ 4\ 3 \\ \hline 7 \\ 6\ 0 \\ \hline 6\ 7 \end{array}
$$

Learning Tasks 2-3, p. 29
Have the student rewrite the problems vertically, aligning the digits in the proper columns. If necessary, use graph paper, or notebook paper turned sideways, to help align the digits. Point out that though this seems a longer way to do addition than what she is used to, this method will be useful when the numbers get larger with more places.

2. **57**

3. (a) **69**   (b) **79**   (c) **58**

    (d) **69**   (e) **94**   (f) **99**

Workbook Exercise 11

(14) Addition within 1000 (pp. 29-30)

> ➢ Add a 2-digit or 3-digit number to a 3-digit number without renaming.
> ➢ Solve word problems involving addition within 1000.

➤ Use a place value chart and number discs to illustrate
addition of a 3-digit number to a 2-digit number, and
then a 3-digit number to another 3-digit number, where
there is no renaming.

```
    6 3 7
  +   2 2
    6 5 9

    2 2 5
  + 3 6 2
    5 8 7
```

Page 28
Discuss this page. You should already have illustrated this procedure with
number discs. Your student should be able to relate this process to a variety of
base-10 material, so if he has trouble with this page, illustrate it with number
discs, money, or other objects where one object represents 10 times as much
as another object, such as bundles of toothpicks.

Learning Tasks 4-6, pp. 29-30
Use number discs or base-10 blocks to illustrate these problems if necessary.
Have your student rewrite the addition problems in task 6 vertically, being
careful to align the digits properly. Use graph paper or notebook paper turned
sideways if necessary.

4. **285**

5. **387**

6. (a) **134**   (b) **290**   (c) **197**
    (d) **589**   (e) **576**   (f) **595**

Learning Task 7, p. 30
Once your student is able to align the problems vertically, do not insist that he
rewrite problems vertically on paper for all problems if he can align them
mentally and get the correct answer. You may want to ask your student to
name the parts and explain why we add to solve this problem (we need to find
the whole, or total).

7. **189**

 Workbook Exercise 12

Part 3 – Subtraction without Renaming

(15) Vertical Subtraction of 2-Digit Numbers (pp. 31-32)

- ➢ Subtract ones, tens, or hundreds.
- ➢ Subtract within 100, without renaming, using the formal algorithm for addition.

 Learning Task 1, p. 32
It is not necessary to rewrite these vertically unless your students still needs help aligning digits. The point of the task is to note the place value of the digits. Ones are subtracted from ones, tens from tens, and hundreds from hundreds.

1. (a) **4**   (b) **40**   (c) **400**

➤ Tell your student that he is going to learn to subtract numbers larger than 100. Use number discs and a **place-value chart**. Write a subtraction equation for 2-digit numbers in vertical format (no renaming).

Ask your student to place the first number of discs on the place-value chart. Say "5 ones minus 3 ones is 2 ones." Ask your student to remove the appropriate number of ones. Show him that we write the answer in the ones place under the line. Then say "6 tens minus 4 tens is 2 tens." Ask your student to remove appropriate number of tens. Show him that we write the answer in the tens place under the column of tens digits. Ask for the answer to 65 – 43.

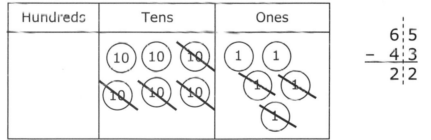

 Learning Task 2-3, p. 32
Have your student rewrite the problems vertically, aligning the digits in the proper columns.

2. **24**

3. (a) **74**   (b) **38**   (c) **60**   (d) **15**   (e) **22**   (f) **10**

📖 **Workbook Exercise 13**

(16) Subtraction within 1000 (pp. 32-33)

  ➤ Subtract a 2-digit or 3-digit number from a 3-digit number without renaming.
➤ Solve word problems involving subtraction within 1000.

➤ Use a place value chart and number discs to illustrate subtraction of a 2-digit number from a 3-digit number, and then a 3-digit number from another 3-digit number, where there is no renaming.

$$
\begin{array}{r}
6\ 3\ 7 \\
-\ \ \ 1\ 2 \\
\hline
6\ 2\ 5
\end{array}
$$

$$
\begin{array}{r}
7\ 9\ 8 \\
-\ 3\ 6\ 2 \\
\hline
4\ 3\ 6
\end{array}
$$

Page 31

Discuss the steps for this problem. You should have already illustrated the steps with actual discs before examining this pictorial representation. It is important that your student first have a concrete introduction to new material; pictures in the textbook are static and do not always convey what is happening.

Learning Tasks 4-7, pp. 32-33

Have your student rewrite the addition problem vertically, being careful to align the digits properly. Let your student work out the problems in task 6 with number discs, if necessary.

4. **214**

5. **224**

6. (a) **406**   (b) **78**
   (c) **512**   (d) **207**
   (e) **220**   (f) **326**

7. **235**

 Workbook Exercise 14

(17) Practice (p. 34)

➢ Practice addition and subtraction, without renaming, within 100.
➢ Solve word problems involving addition and subtraction within 100.

You may want to do all or part of this practice and the next as a lesson with your student, or save it for review later as your student works on other topics. If your student has been doing Primary Mathematics for a while, she may be able to do the calculations mentally. If she gets any wrong, you may want to have her write the problem vertically if she did not solve it that way. Make sure she is aligning the digits properly and adding or subtracting the digits in the same place for each number.

Practice 2A

1. (a) **37**   (b) **76**   (c) **88**

2. (a) **61**   (b) **39**   (c) **51**

3. (a) **77**   (b) **99**   (c) **98**

4. (a) **20**   (b) **36**   (c) **22**

5. (a) **89**   (b) **40**   (c) **5**

6.   36 - 11 = **25**

stamps Devi had 36	
given away 11	left ?

7.   43 + 24 = **67**

chicken satay 43	beef satay 24
total ?	

8.   48 - 25 = **23**

comparison

US› cherries, 3d› rambutans 48	
US› kiwis, 3d› chikus 25	more ?

9.   23 + 76 = **99**

sold in morning 23	sold in afternoon 76
total ?	

10. $19 - $14 = **$5**

cost of book $19	
money she has $14	money she needs ?

(18) Practice (p. 35)

> Practice addition and subtraction, without renaming, within 1000.
> Solve word problems involving addition and subtraction within 1000.

Practice 2B

1. (a) **359**   (b) **168**   (c) **599**
2. (a) **862**   (b) **622**   (c) **441**
3. (a) **193**   (b) **567**   (c) **597**
4. (a) **528**   (b) **294**   (c) **224**
5. (a) **488**   (b) **502**   (c) **607**

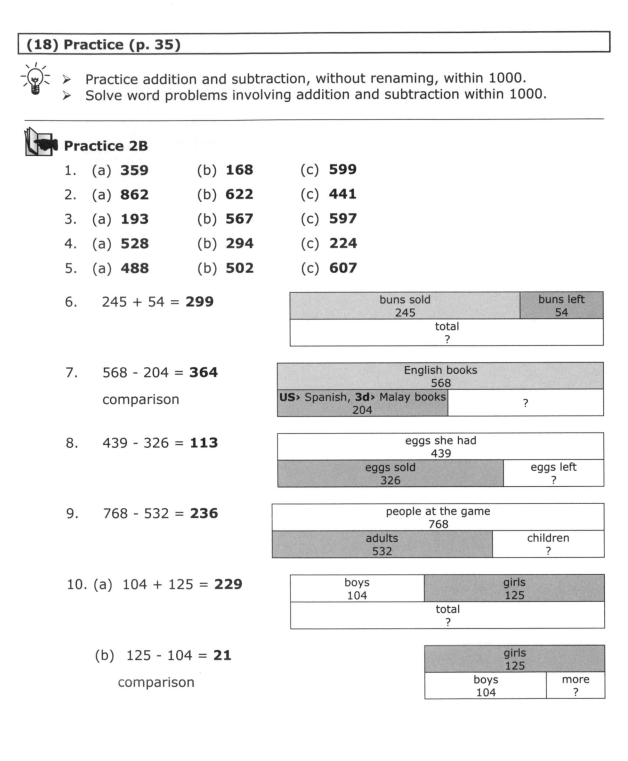

6. 245 + 54 = **299**

buns sold 245	buns left 54
total ?	

7. 568 - 204 = **364**

    comparison

English books 568	
US› Spanish, 3d› Malay books 204	?

8. 439 - 326 = **113**

eggs she had 439	
eggs sold 326	eggs left ?

9. 768 - 532 = **236**

people at the game 768	
adults 532	children ?

10. (a) 104 + 125 = **229**

boys 104	girls 125
total ?	

    (b) 125 - 104 = **21**

    comparison

girls 125	
boys 104	more ?

Renaming

These games are meant to introduce addition and subtraction with renaming. You can do these games as part of the lesson, and have your student do the practice independently, or you can save them for the next section.

Material: **Place-value charts** for each player, 4 sets of **number cards 0-9** (a deck of playing cards with face cards removed and tens made into 0's), **number discs** (1's, 10's, 100's) or base-10 blocks.

Game 1: Set a target number such as 900. Players take turns drawing a card. They place the same number of ones on their chart as the number on the card. Whenever there are 10 in a column for one place (ones or tens) they need to be traded in for a disc or block of next higher place value. The first student who reaches the target number (at the end of a round) wins. If several students have reached the target number in the round, the one closest wins.

Game 2: Use starting number such as 900 or 555. Students should each place that number on their place-value chart using the discs or blocks. Players take turns drawing a card. They remove the same number of ones from their place-value chart as the number on the card. Whenever there are not enough ones, they trade in a ten for 10 ones. Whenever there are not enough tens, they trade in a hundred for 10 tens. The first player for which there are not enough discs to remove (the number drawn is higher than the number of ones left on the chart) wins. If several players reach this stage in a round, the one with the least number of ones remaining wins.

Part 4 – Addition with Renaming

In this section the student will learn to add numbers of up to 3-digits using the formal algorithm for addition.

In the formal algorithm for addition, the problem is worked in a vertical format where the digits are aligned in columns for each place. A line is drawn under the numbers to separate the sum from the numbers being added.

First the ones are added. If the sum is 10 ones or more, it is renamed as tens and ones, and the ones are written down under the line in the ones place (under the column of ones).

$$\begin{array}{r} \mathbf{1} \\ 5\ 6\ 7 \\ +\quad 2\ 3\ 5 \\ \hline \downarrow\ \mathbf{2} \end{array}$$

Then the tens are added, including any renamed ten. If the sum is 10 tens (100) or more, it is renamed as hundreds and tens, and the tens written down in the tens place under the line.

$$\begin{array}{r} \mathbf{1}\ 1\ \\ 5\ 6\ 7 \\ +\quad 2\ 3\ 5 \\ \hline \mathbf{0}\ 2 \\ \downarrow \end{array}$$

Then the hundreds are added. This process is illustrated with number discs on p. 28 of the textbook for a situation where there is no renaming, and on p. 36 where ones are renamed.

$$\begin{array}{r} \mathbf{1}\ 1\ \\ 5\ 6\ 7 \\ +\quad 2\ 3\ 5 \\ \hline \mathbf{8}\ 0\ 2 \end{array}$$

All the learning task problems in the text for this unit should be rewritten vertically to illustrate the algorithm. For some of the tasks, you may also want to discuss mental math techniques. Your student may be able apply mental math techniques to the addition or subtraction of 3-digit numbers with renaming in some cases. Additional strategies will be given in *Primary Mathematics 2B* and *Primary Mathematics 3B*. Do not insist on a particular strategy when students are working on their own. Allow students to develop flexibility in working with numbers through experimenting with different ways of regrouping. They should develop their own criteria for which problems are easier to solve using the formal algorithm and which can be solved mentally or with an alternate strategy. The formal algorithm is a fail-safe strategy that will always work. The advantage to starting with the ones is that it avoids retracing steps. Once the ones are found, they will never change. Then when the tens are found next, they too will not change. In adding hundreds first, adding tens or even ones might change the hundreds.

(19) Renaming Ones in 2-Digit Addition (pp. 36-37)

- ➤ Add ones or tens where there is renaming once.
- ➤ Add numbers within 100 where the ones are renamed using the formal algorithm for addition.

Learning Task 1, p. 37
(Save p. 36 until after learning task 1)

Use number discs or base-10 blocks and a place-value chart to illustrate these tasks. A suggested procedure is given here following the answers.

1. (a) **13** (b) **69** (c) **73** (d) **130** (e) **609** (f) **730**

Ask your student for the answer to 1(a), 1(b), and 1(c). Ask him to explain how he arrived at the answer. He may have used a mental math method, such as making a ten:
- 64 needs 6 more to make 70. Take 6 from the 9 leaving 3.
  64 + 9 = 70 + 3 = 73
- Make a ten with the 9 by taking it from the 4.
  64 + 9 = 60 + 10 + 3 = 73

Rewrite the problem vertically, and illustrate with a place-value chart and number discs: 4 ones + 9 ones = 13 ones. Replace the 13 ones with 1 ten and 3 ones. Tell her that we show this by writing the renamed ten above the tens and the total number of ones under the other ones. We then add the tens, including the renamed ten, and write the total under the line in the tens place.

Hundreds	Tens	Ones
	⑩ ⑩ ⑩ ⑩ ⑩ ⑩ ⑩	① ① ① ① ① ① ① ① ① ① ① ① ①

$$\begin{array}{r} {\scriptstyle 1} \\ 6\ 4 \\ +\quad 9 \\ \hline 7\ 3 \end{array}$$

Do some additional problems where a 1-digit number is added to a 2-digit number with renaming. Allow your student to solve in different ways, but illustrate the formal algorithm each time.

Have your student solve 1(d). 4 tens + 9 tens = 13 tens. Place 13 1-discs on the chart. Elicit the answer to 13 tens = _____ hundreds _____ tens. Write some similar renaming problems.

12 tens = _____ hundreds _____ tens
35 tens = _____ hundreds _____ tens
40 tens = _____ hundreds _____ tens

Have your student solve 1(e). Illustrate with number discs, if necessary. Do some additional problems where a 1-digit number is added to a 3-digit number, including some where there is renaming of the ones, e.g. 459 + 3. Students may also solve these mentally.

Discuss 1(f) and illustrate with number discs. Discuss various approaches.
- Rewrite the problem vertically, and add the tens, then the hundreds, including the renamed hundred.
- Make a hundred. Take 70 from the 70 to bring 640 to 700, add the remaining 30.
  640 + 90 = 700 + 30 = 730
- Make 100 with 90.
  640 + 90 = 630 + 100 = 730
- Look at the hundreds. 6 hundreds + 0 hundreds = 6 hundreds. Before writing 6, look ahead. There will be another 100, so write down 7 instead. Add the tens. Look ahead to see if there will be another ten. There is not, so write down the total tens. Write down a 0 for ones.

$$\begin{array}{r} 1 \\ 6\ 4\ 0 \\ +\quad 9\ 0 \\ \hline 7\ 3\ 0 \end{array}$$

There are additional problems involving adding tens with renaming in Mental Math 11 that may be done now or later for review.

Page 36
Illustrate the steps in this problem with concrete number discs and a place-value chart.

Learning Task 2, p. 37
Illustrate as many problems as necessary with number discs, making sure your student sees the connection between the process and each step of the written representation.

2. (a) **42**   (b) **80**   (c) **86**   (d) **83**   (e) **70**   (f) **100**

 Workbook Exercise 15

(20) Renaming Ones in 3-Digit Addition (pp. 37-38)

 ➤ Add numbers within 1000 where the ones are renamed using the formal algorithm for addition.

 Learning Tasks 3-6, pp. 37-38
Illustrate these problems as needed with **number discs** correlating each action using the number discs with the written representation. It is important that your student see the process step-by-step rather than just the static picture in the textbook. Have your student rewrite the problems in tasks 4 and 6 vertically, making sure she aligns the digits properly.

3. **361**
4. (a) **323**   (b) **231**   (c) **572**   (d) **656**   (e) **770**   (f) **390**
5. **390**
6. (a) **492**   (b) **671**   (c) **763**   (d) **881**   (e) **610**   (f) **990**

➤ Your student may be able to do 4(a) and 4(b) mentally. 315 + 8, for example, can be done by writing down the 3 for the hundreds, and then mentally adding 15 + 8 using techniques learned in *Primary Mathematics 1*. There is additional practice in Mental Math 12 that you may have your student do now or later.

Workbook Exercises 16, #1

---

(21) Renaming Tens (pp. 38-39)

 ➢ Add numbers within 1000 where the tens are renamed using the formal algorithm for addition.

 Learning Tasks 7-10, pp. 38-39
It is important to illustrate as many of these problems as needed with number discs so that your student can see each step rather than just the static pictures in tasks 7 and 8. Have your student rewrite the problems in tasks 8 and 10 vertically, making sure he aligns the digits properly. Allow your student to use number discs for tasks 7 and 8 if needed.

7. **619**
8. (a) **352**   (b) **644**   (c) **448**   (d) **724**   (e) **500**   (f) **309**
9. **527**
10. (a) **617**   (b) **826**   (c) **608**   (d) **808**   (e) **618**   (f) **929**

 Workbook Exercises 16, #2
Workbook Exercise 17

Your student may not be able to do all these problems in one sitting. You may wish to allow two days for these exercises, or save some of the problems to combine with some of the problems in Exercises 18 -19 for an extra day, using the following game and problems in Practice 2C as material for a lesson.

Reach 100

Materials: **Number cube 1-6**, paper and pencil, **pennies** and **dimes** (or number discs).

Procedure: Each player takes turns rolling the number cube. The player must decide to get either dimes or pennies for the number rolled. Any time he has ten pennies he must trade it in for a dime. Each player rolls 7 times. The player whose money is closest to $1.00 after 7 rolls wins.

Variation: Use paper turned sideways or make 2 columns.
Each player takes turns rolling the number cubes. The player must determine whether to place the number rolled in the tens place or the ones place. If he chooses to make it a ten, he writes a 0 after it. Each player rolls 7 times. The numbers are added up and the player closest to 100 after 7 rolls wins.

(22) Renaming Ones and Tens (pp. 39-40)

➢ Add numbers within 1000 where renaming occurs twice.

➤ Use **base-10 blocks** and the **place-value chart** to illustrate addition with renaming using 3-digit numbers where the sum of the ones and the tens needs to be renamed, as in learning tasks 11 and 13 on pages 39 and 40. You can either illustrate the problems in the text, or illustrate the problem below, and then proceed to the pictures in the text. Some students may not need to use the discs any more, but others may still need them to do the problems. Allow your student to use the discs and place-value chart when needed.

Write

$$\begin{array}{r} 167 \\ + 285 \end{array}$$

Put 1 hundred, 6 tens, and 7 ones on the chart, and then 2 hundreds, 8 tens, and 5 ones below. Add the ones (7 ones + 5 ones = 12 ones). Rename the ones (12 ones = 1 ten + 2 ones). Trade in ten ones for a ten and put the new ten in the tens column.

$$\begin{array}{r} 1 \\ 167 \\ + 285 \\ \hline 2 \end{array}$$

Write a 1 above the tens column to show the renamed ten. Write a 2 in the ones column to show how many ones total there are.

Add the tens (1 ten + 6 tens + 8 tens = 15 tens). There are 15 tens. Rename them (15 tens = 1 hundred 5 tens), and replace 10 tens on the chart with a hundred and place it in the hundreds column.

$$\begin{array}{r} 1\,1 \\ 167 \\ + 285 \\ \hline 52 \end{array}$$

Write a 1 above the hundreds column to show the renamed hundred, and a 5 under the tens to show the total tens.

$$\begin{array}{r} 1\,1 \\ 167 \\ + 285 \\ \hline 452 \end{array}$$

Add the hundreds (1 hundred + 1 hundred + 2 hundreds = 4 hundreds) and write 4 in the hundreds column.

Learning Tasks 11-14, pp. 39-40

Have your student rewrite the problems in tasks 12 and 14 vertically. Give him additional problems or examples if necessary.

12. (a) **334**   (b) **521**   (c) **703**

13. **421**

14. (a) **621**   (b) **602**   (c) **600**

📖 **Workbook Exercise 18**

(23) Adding 3 Numbers (p. 40)

 ➢ Add 3 numbers within 1000.

Learning Tasks 15-16, p. 40
Use **number discs** and the **place-value chart** to illustrate the learning tasks. Have your student rewrite the problems in task 16 vertically.

16. (a) **733**   (b) **921**

 Add 3 Digits

Material: Playing cards with tens and face cards removed.

Procedure: Cards are shuffled and placed face down in the middle.
o Game 1 – Each player draws 8 cards and arranges the cards into two 3-digit numbers and one 2-digit number and adds them together. The player with the *lowest* sum wins.
o Game 2 – The dealer deals 6 cards to each player. The players arrange their cards into three 2-digit numbers and add them together. The player with the *lowest* sum wins.

Workbook Exercise 19

(24) Practice (p. 41)

➢ Practice addition within 100.

Your student can do this and the next practice independently, or you can do some of the word problems as part of the lesson, as well as some of the game suggestions. The games can be done at any time for additional practice.

 Practice 2C

1. (a) **35**   (b) **40**   (c) **53**
2. (a) **63**   (b) **80**   (c) **90**
3. (a) **100**   (b) **100**   (c) **100**
4. (a) **107**   (b) **115**   (c) **119**
5. (a) **115**   (b) **129**   (c) **109**
6. 92 - 42 = **50**
7. 86 + 22 = **108**
8. 58 - 42 = **16**
9. 18 + 26 = **44**
10. (a) 46 + 28 = **74**
    (b) 74 + 16 = **90**
         or 46 + 28 + 16 = **90**

Get the Number

Material: Deck of **playing cards** with tens and face cards removed.

Single player: Shuffle cards. Turn over 2 cards. The first card is the ten and the second card is the ones of the target number. Turn over the next 4 cards. Arrange the cards as two 2-digit numbers so that the sum will be as close to the target number as possible. Repeat with a new target number.

Multi-player: After the target number is determined, deal 4 cards to each player. The player whose sum is closest wins.

(25) Practice (p. 41)

➢ Practice addition within 1000.

Practice, p. 41

1. (a) **314**   (b) **439**   (c) **435**
2. (a) **445**   (b) **580**   (c) **693**
3. (a) **853**   (b) **951**   (c) **894**
4. (a) **629**   (b) **834**   (c) **895**
5. (a) **377**   (b) **483**   (c) **650**
6. 169 + 71 = **240**
7. 240 + 85 = **325**
8. 102 + 86 + 40 = **228**
9. 285 - 70 = **215**
10. $125 + $36 = **$161**

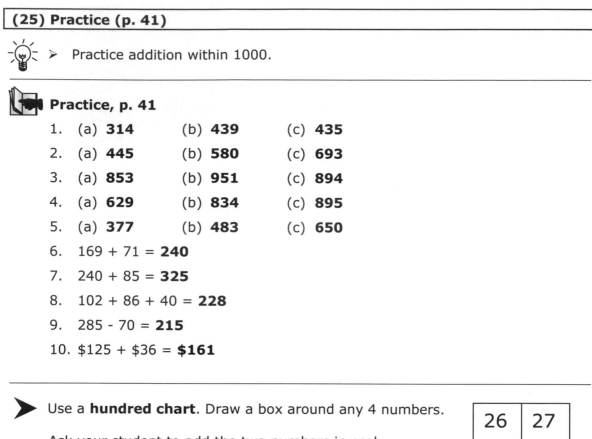

➤ Use a **hundred chart**. Draw a box around any 4 numbers.

Ask your student to add the two numbers in each diagonal.
        26 + 37 = ?, 36 + 27 = ?
Ask him to describe anything he notices. (The totals are the same.)

26	27
36	37

Draw a box around any nine numbers.

Ask your student to add the three numbers in each diagonal.
        57 + 68 + 79 = ?, 77 + 68 + 59 = ?
Do they also have the same total?

57	58	59
67	68	69
77	78	79

Try it with another group of nine numbers. Does it work with a group of 16 numbers?

Try the same thing with a calendar.

Discuss why the total of the numbers for both diagonals is the same.

Reach 1000

Materials: **Number cube 1-6**

Procedure: Turn lined paper sideways or draw three columns. Each player takes turns rolling the number cube. The player must determine whether to place the number rolled in the hundreds place, the tens place, or the ones place. Each player rolls 7 times. The numbers are added up and the player whose sum is closest to 1000 wins.

Get the Number

Material: Deck of **playing cards** with tens and face cards removed.

Single player: Shuffle cards. Turn over 3 cards. The first card is the hundreds, the second card is the tens, and the third card is the ones of the target number. Turn over the next 6 cards. Arrange the cards as two 3-digit numbers so that the sum will be as close to the target number as possible. Repeat with a new target number.

Multi-player: After the target number is determined, deal 6 cards to each player. The player whose sum is closest wins.

Part 5 – Subtraction with Renaming

In this section the student will learn to subtract numbers of up to 3-digits using the formal algorithm for subtraction.

In the subtraction algorithm, the problem is worked in a vertical format.

First, the ones must be subtracted. If there are not enough ones in the top number to subtract from, a ten is renamed as 10 ones and added to the ones in the top number. There is now one less ten. The ones are subtracted and the difference written under the line in the ones place.

$$
\begin{array}{r}
2 \\
8\ \ \cancel{3}\ ^1 2 \\
-\ 6\ 7\ 9 \\
\hline
3
\end{array}
$$

Then, the tens must be subtracted. If there are not enough tens in the top number to subtract from, a hundred is renamed as 10 tens and added to the tens in the top number. There is now one less hundred. The tens are subtracted and the difference written under the line in the tens place.

$$
\begin{array}{r}
7\ ^1 2 \\
\cancel{8}\ \cancel{3}\ ^1 2 \\
-\ 6\ 7\ 9 \\
\hline
5\ 3
\end{array}
$$

Then the hundreds are subtracted.

$$
\begin{array}{r}
7\ ^1 2 \\
\cancel{8}\ \cancel{3}\ ^1 2 \\
-\ 6\ 7\ 9 \\
\hline
1\ 5\ 3
\end{array}
$$

All the learning task problems in the text for this unit should be rewritten vertically to illustrate the algorithm. For some of the tasks, you may also want to discuss mental math techniques. Your student may be able apply mental math techniques to the addition or subtraction of 3-digit numbers with renaming in some cases. Allow your student to use whatever method he prefers, but make sure he understands how to subtract using the formal algorithm. This method will always work, and does not require retracing steps of changing answers in each place.

(26) Renaming Tens in 2-Digit Subtraction (pp. 43-44)

 ➢ Subtract ones or tens where there is renaming once.
➢ Subtract numbers within 100 where the tens are renamed using the formal algorithm for subtraction.

Learning Task 1, p. 44
(Save p. 43 until after learning task 1)

Use **number discs** or **base-10 blocks** and a **place-value chart** to illustrate these tasks. A suggested procedure is given here following the answers.

1.   (a) **4**   (b) **5**   (c) **35**   (d) **40**   (e) **50**   (f) **350**

Ask your student for the answers to 1(a) through 1(c). Have him explain how he found the answer. Students who have done *Primary Mathematics 1* may solve (b) and (c) by subtracting from a ten.
• For 41 – 6, take 6 from a ten, leaving 4 ones.
  41 – 6 = 31 + 10 – 6 = 31 + 4 = 35

Illustrate how to solve 1(c) using number discs and the formal algorithm for subtraction. Rewrite the problem vertically. Place 4 tens and 1 one on the place-value chart. Ask your students how we can get enough ones from which to subtract 6. Replace a ten with ten ones and show how this is represented by crossing out the 4, writing a 3 above it, and putting a 1 next to the 1 to show that we have 11 ones, or crossing it out and writing 11 above it. Then remove 6 ones, say, "11 ones minus 6 ones is 5 ones," and write 5 below the line in the ones place. Write the remaining 3 tens below the line in the tens place.

$$\begin{array}{r} \overset{3}{\cancel{4}}\,{}^{1}1 \\ -\quad 6 \\ \hline 3\;\;5 \end{array}$$

Ask your student to answer 1(d) through 1(f). Ask him how we can get enough tens from which to subtract 6 tens. Illustrate 1(f) with number discs, and show how we represent the renaming on paper. Discuss other approaches, if desired:

$$\begin{array}{r} \overset{3}{\cancel{4}}\,{}^{1}1\;\;0 \\ -\quad 6\;\;0 \\ \hline 3\;\;5\;\;0 \end{array}$$

• Subtract from a 100
  410 – 60 = 310 + 100 – 60 = 310 + 40 = 350
• Before writing down the hundreds, look ahead to see if there will be enough tens to subtract from. There are not, so write down one less hundred. Subtract 6 tens from 100, add the resulting 4 tens to the ten, and write down 5 tens. Write down a 0 for ones.

You may wish to have your student practice mental subtraction of tens now or at a later time. There is additional practice in Mental Math 13-15.

Page 43
Show your student the step with actual discs and place-value chart, not just by looking at the picture.

Note that in the text, the ones are crossed out, and 12 is written above. The steps can also be shown by writing a little 1 in front of the 2 to show that we now have 12 ones.

$$
\begin{array}{r}
\overset{5}{\cancel{6}}\,{}^{1}2 \\
-\ 4\ 3 \\
\hline
1\ 9
\end{array}
$$

Learning Task 2, p. 44
Illustrate as many problems as necessary with number discs, making sure your student sees the connection between the process and each step of the written representation.

2.   (a) **24**   (b) **32**   (c) **39**

   (d) **28**   (e) **26**   (f) **28**

 Workbook Exercise 20, #1

(27) Practice (p. 48)

> Practice subtraction within 100.

In Practice 2E, only 2-digit numbers are involved, so you may do this practice before moving on to subtracting 3-digit numbers.

Practice 2E

1. (a)   **32** (b)   **38** (c)   **36**
2. (a)   **27** (b)   **29** (c)   **25**
3. (a)   **18** (b)   **48** (c)   **45**
4. (a)   **9**   (b)   **7**   (c)   **1**
5. (a)   **5**   (b)   **5**   (c)   **5**

6.   18 + 14 = **32**

Ailian's books 18	14
Devi's books ?	

7.   92 - 9 = **83**

comparison

Jenny's shells 92	
Mary's shells ?	9

8.   84 - 15 = **69**

T-shirts bought 84	
given to friends 15	left ?

9. $92 - $58 = **$34**

total money $92	
money spent $58	money left ?

10. $42 + $28 = **$70**

cost of dictionary $42	money left $28
total money ?	

Get the Number (tens)

Material: Deck of **playing cards** with tens and face cards removed.

Single player: Shuffle cards. Turn over 2 cards. The first card is the ten and the second card is the ones of the target number. Turn over the next 4 cards. Arrange the cards as two 2-digit numbers so that the difference will be as close to the target number as possible. For example, the target number is 45. A player turns over 9, 3, 5, and 1. He or she can form the two numbers 93 and 51 and subtract them to get 42, which is 3 less than the target number. Repeat with a new target number.

Multi-player: After the target number is determined, deal 4 cards to each player. The player whose difference is closest to the target number wins.

Reach 0

Materials: **Number cube 1-6**, paper and pencil, **pennies** and **dimes** (or 1-discs and 10-discs).

Procedure: Players start with 10 dimes. Each player takes turns rolling the number cube. The player must decide to remove dimes or pennies for the number rolled. Whenever he doesn't have enough pennies, he must trade a dime in for pennies. Each player rolls 7 times. If the player does not have enough money to subtract the amount rolled, he must add back dimes according to the number of rolled. For example, the player rolls a 4 and a 5 and takes away 9 dimes. He then rolls a 6 and trades in the remaining dime for pennies, takes away 6 pennies, and has 4 left. On his next roll, his fourth, he rolls a 5. He doesn't have enough pennies, so must add back in 5 dimes. The player with the least money left after 7 rolls wins.

Variation: Use paper turned sideways to make columns or draw two columns. Write 100 at the top of the columns. The player must determine after each roll of the number cube whether to place the number rolled in the tens place or the ones place. If he chooses to make it a ten, he writes a 0 after it. He subtracts that number from the previous number. Each player rolls 7 times. If he doesn't have enough left to subtract the number rolled, he must add the same number of tens as the number rolled. The player with the lowest number after 7 rolls wins.

(28) Renaming Tens in 3-Digit Subtraction (pp. 44-45)

➢ Subtract from a 3-digit number when tens are renamed.
➢ Subtract from a 3-digit number when hundreds are renamed.

Learning Tasks 3-6, pp. 44-45
Have the student rewrite the problem vertically. Illustrate the steps with **number discs**, relating each step done with the number discs to each step done in the written format. Do additional examples if necessary.

3. **225**

4. (a) **345**   (b) **473**   (c) **528**   (d) **645**   (e) **702**   (f) **804**

5. **318**

6. (a) **214**   (b) **325**   (c) **258**   (d) **214**   (e) **507**   (f) **106**

➤ The exercises mix up problems involving renaming tens or hundreds. If your student is doing well, combine this lesson with the next lesson and do some of the next lesson's workbook problems. Otherwise, provide more practice with subtraction of numbers within 1000 where only tens are renamed.

Your student may be able to subtract a 1-digit number from a 3-digit number using mental calculations, or by leaving the problem in its horizontal format. For example, 354 – 9 can be done by writing down the 3 for the hundreds, then doing 54 – 9 mentally. One way to do this is to first write down the 3 (**3**_ _). Then, before writing down the tens, look ahead to see if a ten will need to be renamed. If it does, then write down one less ten (**34**_). Then determine the ones either by subtracting 9 from a 10 and adding the result to 4, or recalling the subtraction fact for 14 – 9, and writing down the ones (34**5**). For this particular problem, the student could do it by subtracting ten and then adding 1. There is additional practice in Mental Math 16 and 17, which can be done now or later.

(29) Renaming Hundreds (pp. 45-46)

 ➢ Subtract from a 3-digit number when hundreds are renamed.

 Learning Tasks 7-10, pp. 45-46
Have the student rewrite the problem vertically. Illustrate the steps with **number discs** or base-10 blocks. Do additional examples if necessary.

7. **665**

8. (a) **272**   (b) **371**   (c) **462**   (d) **646**   (e) **540**   (f) **56**

9. **245**

10. (a) **370**   (b) **168**   (c) **213**   (d) **321**   (e) **350**   (f) **80**

Reach 0

Materials: **Number cubes**, paper and pencil, **number discs.**

Procedure: Each player starts with 10 hundreds. The players take turns rolling the number cube. After each roll, the players must decide whether the number rolled should be a hundred, a ten, or a one. They must take away the corresponding number from the number from their discs, renaming a hundred as 10 tens or a ten as 10 ones to do so. Each player rolls 7 times. If a player does not have enough money to subtract the amount rolled, he adds back in the same number of 100 discs as the number rolled. After 7 rolls, the player closest to 0 wins.

Variation: Record the results on paper rather than using base-10 material. Players write the starting number, 1000, and then write down the ones, tens, or hundreds they roll and subtract from their previous answer.

Workbook Exercise 20, #2-5
Workbook Exercise 21

Your student may not be able to do all these problems in one sitting. You may wish to allow two days for these exercises, or save some of the problems to do later as review.

(30) Renaming Tens and Hundreds (pp. 46-47)

 ➢ Subtract from a 3-digit number when renaming occurs twice.

Learning Tasks 11-14, pp. 46-47
Use actual **number discs** to illustrate tasks 11 and 13. Allow your student to use number discs for tasks 12 and 14, if needed. She should rewrite the problems vertically, aligning the digits correctly.

11. **353**

12. (a) **275**   (b) **375**   (c) **553**

13. **186**

14. (a) **363**   (b) **364**   (c) **377**

Workbook Exercise 22

(31) Subtraction with No Tens (p. 47)

➢ Subtracting 3-digit numbers where there are no ones or tens.

Use **base-10 blocks** or number discs and a **place-value chart** to illustrate subtraction of 3-digit numbers when there are not enough ones and no tens, with renaming twice, as in learning task 15 on p. 47. To subtract ones, since there aren't any tens, a hundred has to be renamed as 9 tens and 10 ones.

Before using the text, you can give your student a problem, such as 400 – 345, and ask your student how he would solve it. Let him discuss his methods before showing him the standard method.

Learning Tasks 15-16, p. 47
Have the student rewrite the problem vertically. Let him use **base-10 blocks** to solve if necessary. Do additional examples if necessary. Provide additional practice if necessary.

15. 272

16. (a) 362   (b) 424   (c) 65

Workbook Exercises 23-24.
The next few lessons involve practices in the text. You may want to do the word problems as part of a lesson and then assign exercise 24 as homework, or allow two days for these exercises.

(32) Practice (p. 49)

- ➢ Practice subtraction within 1000.
- ➢ Solve word problems involving addition and subtraction within 100.

Practice 2F (except for 10(b)) covers 3-digit subtraction.

Practice 2F

1. (a) **320**   (b) **432**   (c) **540**
2. (a) **77**   (b) **308**   (c) **425**
3. (a) **162**   (b) **207**   (c) **207**
4. (a) **391**   (b) **394**   (c) **394**
5. (a) **177**   (b) **416**   (c) **77**
6. 320 - 180 = **140**
7. 224 + 298 = **522**
8. 105 - 87 = **18**
9. 620 - 465 = **155**
10. (a)   304 - 46 = **258**
    (b)   304 + 258 = **562**

Subtraction

Material: Deck of playing cards with face cards removed and tens marked as 0 (or four sets of number cards 0-9)

Game 1: The dealer shuffles the cards and turns over the first three cards. The first card is the hundreds, the second card is the tens and the third card is the ones of the target number. The dealer then deals six cards to each player. The players arrange their cards in to two 3-digit numbers so that the difference will be as close to the target number as possible. The winner is the player whose difference is the closest to the target number.

Game 2: The dealer deals 6 cards to each player. The players arrange their cards into two 3-digit numbers and subtract. The player with the *lowest* difference wins. You may want to help your student explore how to arrange the numbers to get the lowest answer.

(33) Practice (p. 50)

> Practice addition and subtraction within 1000.
> Solve word problems involving addition and subtraction within 1000.

Practices 2G and 2H cover both addition and subtraction. You many want to save 2G and 2H to do at a later date as a review.

Practice 2G

1. (a) **79**   (b) **79**   (c) **99**
2. (a) **59**   (b) **40**   (c) **6**
3. (a) **108**   (b) **80**   (c) **109**
4. (a) **33**   (b) **35**   (c) **5**
5. (a) **100**   (b) **101**   (c) **107**
6. 98 - 39 = **59**
7. 82 + 24 = **106**
8. (a) Team B
   (b) 95 - 79 = **16**
9. (a) 26 + 9 = **35**
   (b) 35 + 8 = **43**

Hundreds

Material: **3 number cubes**, paper and pencil

Single player: Roll the three number cubes twice. On the first roll, make the largest 3-digit number possible, and on the second roll the smallest. The player must then subtract the two. His answer is his score for that roll. Continue, adding the score after each turn, until the scores add to 1000.

Multi-player: Players take turns rolling the number cubes twice, adding their scores after each turn. The first to reach 1,000 wins.

(34) Practice (p. 51)

➤ Practice addition and subtraction within 1000.
➤ Solve word problems involving addition and subtraction within 1000.

Practice 2H

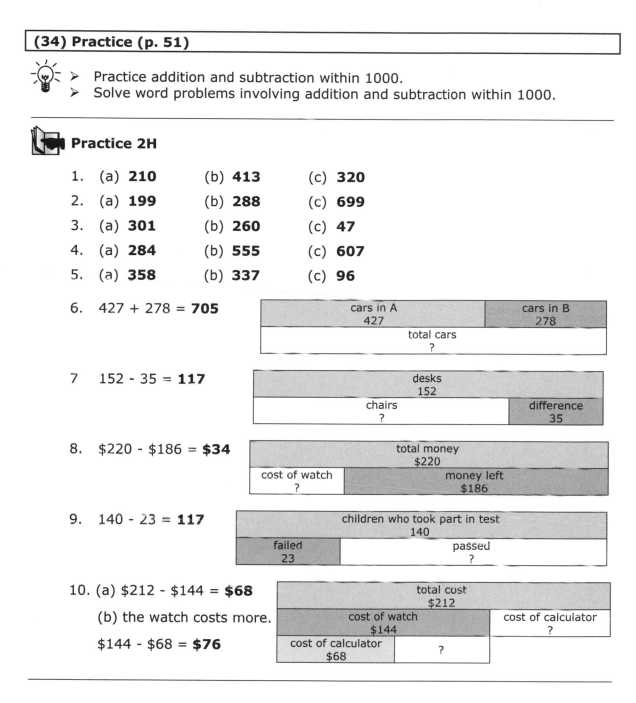

1. (a) **210**   (b) **413**   (c) **320**

2. (a) **199**   (b) **288**   (c) **699**

3. (a) **301**   (b) **260**   (c) **47**

4. (a) **284**   (b) **555**   (c) **607**

5. (a) **358**   (b) **337**   (c) **96**

6. 427 + 278 = **705**

cars in A 427	cars in B 278
total cars ?	

7. 152 - 35 = **117**

desks 152	
chairs ?	difference 35

8. $220 - $186 = **$34**

total money $220	
cost of watch ?	money left $186

9. 140 - 23 = **117**

children who took part in test 140	
failed 23	passed ?

10. (a) $212 - $144 = **$68**

(b) the watch costs more.

$144 - $68 = **$76**

total cost $212	
cost of watch $144	cost of calculator ?
cost of calculator $68	?

(35) Review

➢ Review all topics learned so far in *Primary Mathematics*.

For more practice in mental math, you may want to have your student do Mental Math 18-20. Your student should mentally add or subtract the numbers from left to right, using mental math strategies she has already learned.

Mental Math 21 involves adding or subtracting tens from a 3-digit number and can be done by thinking of the problem such as 241 – 60 as 24 tens – 6 tens; finding the answer as with 24 – 6, then adding on the ones.

Mental Math 22 has a variety of problems.

The Mental Math exercises can be done later for review.

 Workbook Review 1

Unit 3 – Length

Part 1 – Measuring Length in Meters

(36) Meters (pp. 52-53)

- ➢ Understand the meter as a unit of measurement.
- ➢ Estimate the length of an object as equal to, longer than, or shorter than 1 meter.

In *Primary Mathematics 1*, students learned to measure length in non-standard units, such as paper clips. In this unit the standard units of meter and centimeter are introduced.

Units are of vital importance in every civilization as they are an essential means of communication. At one time, sizes of body parts were used as units. However, since people don't share the same body sizes, it was not possible to communicate exact measurements since measured data depended on the measurer.

The original definition of the meter was one ten-millionth of the distance from the North Pole to the Equator. The definition was changed several times. As of 1983 the meter is defined as the length of path traveled by light in vacuum during a time interval of 1 / 299,792,458 of a second.

If you are in the US, your student probably already has some understanding of the standard measurement of yards, feet, or inches. You may wish to explain that the metric system has become the global language of measurement and that today 94.5% of the world's population uses the metric system. The only other countries besides the US that have not officially adopted the metric system are Liberia (in western Africa) and Myanmar (also known as Burma, in Southeast Asia). The use of the metric system is legal (but not mandatory) in the United States.

For reference, 1 meter is a little longer than 1 yard (1 meter = 39.37 inches). It is about half the height of a very tall adult, about the length of a baseball bat, or about the width of a door.

3d› The American spelling for meter and centimeter will be used in this guide, rather than the British spelling (metre and centimetre).

> Discuss with your student the need for a standard unit of measurement. Measure something in your hand spans. Then let your student measure it in her hand span. Discuss situations such as what would happen if a carpenter needed a board that was 8 hand spans in length.

Show your student a **meter stick**. Explain that a meter is a standard unit of measurement in many countries. The length of the meter is the same in all places, so when something is measured in meters in one place it means the same in another place, not like a hand span.

Use the **meter stick** to measure objects around the house and to determine whether they are longer than or shorter than or about 1 meter long.

It is helpful to have a reference when estimating the length of objects. Have your student find a body part that is about a meter long that he can use as a reference, such as the length from the tip of his fingers to somewhere on his other arm or shoulder when both arms are outstretched, or the length from his foot to some distance up his body.

Have your student estimate the length of objects in meters, such as the height of a door or the length of a picnic table or the width of a room, and then measure.

---

p. 52
Learning Tasks 1-2, p. 53
Answers will vary. Substitute objects around the house for classroom items.

Workbook Exercise 25
Answers will vary. Substitute objects around the house for classroom items.

(37) Addition and Subtraction of Meters (p. 54)

➢ Find the total length in meters by addition.
➢ Find the difference in length by subtraction.

Cut two pieces of string or ribbon, one 1 meter long and one 3 meters long. Have your student measure them, lay them end to end, and give the total length. Note that this is similar to the part-whole model for word problems. We have two parts, each string, and want to find the whole.

Then have him lay one above the other with their left edges aligned and give the difference in length. Note that this is similar to the comparison model for word problems. We are finding out how much longer one string is than the other, so we subtract the length of the longer string from the length of the shorter string.

Find two objects whose lengths differ by a few meters but which your student can't lay side by side. Have her measure them with a meter sticks or string cut to meter lengths to the closest meter. Try to use objects that are close to a whole multiple of a meter. Ask her for the total length of the two objects, and how much longer one is than the other.

Learning Tasks 3-5, p. 54

Tell your student that the lengths in the book are not actual lengths, but have been scaled down, just like a map has scaled down distances. The scale is not accurate, so he must find the answer using addition or subtraction, not by measurement in an attempt to determine the scale.

3. (a) **11 m**   (b) **3 m**

4.   **12 m**

5.   **36 m**

Part 2 – Measuring Length in Centimeters

(38) Centimeters (pp. 55-56)

- ➢ Understand the centimeter as a unit of measurement.
- ➢ Estimate and measure lengths to the nearest centimeter.
- ➢ Compare lengths in centimeters.

➤ Use a **ruler** to show your student another standard length, the centimeter. Have him measure lengths of appropriate objects in centimeters. Explain that the longer marks are for the centimeters, and he is to measure to the nearest long mark. (If necessary, use stiff paper, such as a manila folder, or thin cardboard, to make rulers with only the centimeters marked so that the smaller marks for millimeters do not cause confusion at first.) Emphasize that one end of the object should be placed at the zero mark of the ruler. Depending on the ruler, this may not be at the very edge of the ruler. The length of the object may not be a whole number of centimeters. Have your student approximate the length to the nearest centimeter, saying that the length is "about" a certain length in centimeters. Ask your student to estimate the length of some objects before measuring.

Have your student find a convenient body part to use as a reference that is about 1 cm long, such as the width of her thumb. A dime is about 1 cm wide.

Prepare some strips of paper and have your student first estimate their length and then measure their lengths in centimeters. He can also compare the lengths of two of them, saying how much longer or shorter one is than the other. Explain that the term "difference" means how much longer or shorter an object is. He is finding the "difference" between two lengths.

Do a length hunt. Challenge your student to find a length of a specified number of centimeters. For example, ask her to find something that is 15 cm long.

Ask questions such as "If I say that tree is 5, do I mean 5 meters or 5 centimeters?" or "Is this pencil about 15 meters long?"

p. 55
The grasshopper is **2** cm shorter than the fish, and the fish is **2** cm longer than the grasshopper.

Learning Tasks 1-2, p. 56
Answers will vary.

 Workbook Exercise 26

(39) Curved Lines (pp. 57-58)

- ➢ Measure the length of curved lines.
- ➢ Use a measuring tape.
- ➢ Draw a line of a given length in centimeters.

➤ Draw a curved line and ask your student for some suggestions on how to measure its total length – the length it would have if it were pulled out straight. If he doesn't come up with the idea of using a string put a piece of string down in a curve and ask him how he would find out how long it was. Have your student measure the line you drew by first covering the line with **string** and then measuring the string with a **ruler**. Doing this takes a good deal of coordination, so you may have to demonstrate. Put the start of the string at the start of the curved line, and then match it up with the line by laying it along the line and holding it down with your forefingers, moving them along the string. It does not matter if the start comes off the line. The end can be marked with a marker and/or cut.

Help your student use a **measuring tape** to measure parts of his body and yours - wrist, arm length, circumference of head, length of foot, etc. and compare. For example, is the length of his foot the same as the distance around his arm? Show him how to line up the zero mark with a mark on the measuring tape when measuring around an object. It might be easier to show this by measuring around some other object, such your waist, or a tree trunk, before he tries to measure around himself.

 Learning Tasks 3-6, p. 57

3. **14 cm**

4. Line A is **12** cm. Line B is **12** cm. They are the **same length**.

5. **Papaya Road is shortest. Rambutan Road is longest**.

Workbook Exercise 27

(40) Drawing Lines (p. 58)

➢ Draw a straight line of a given length in centimeters.

➤ Use a **ruler**. Have your student practice drawing lines of various lengths. Point out the importance of starting at the zero mark, and keeping the ruler still. Drawing straight lines involves a good deal of coordination.

Challenge your student to draw lines of a certain length, such as 5 cm, without a ruler, using a straight-edge without markings, such as a piece of cardboard. Then have him measure and see how close he came.

 Learning Task 7, p. 55

 Guess the Length

Materials: **Ruler**, paper and pencil.

Players take turns drawing a line. The other players guess the length to the nearest centimeter. They get one point for each centimeter they are off. Scores can be added for each round. The player with the lowest score wins.

📖 **3d› Workbook Exercise 28**

US> Part 3 – Measuring Length in Yards and Feet

(41) Yards and Feet (US› pp. 59-60)

- ➢ Understand the yard and the foot as units of measurement.
- ➢ Estimate and measure lengths to the nearest yard or foot.
- ➢ Compare a yard with a foot.

➤ Tell your student that in the U.S., common units of measurement are yards and feet. Show your student a **yard stick**. Compare its length to a meter stick.

Use a 1-foot long strip of cardboard, or a **ruler**. Show your student what a foot is. Point out that we say 1 foot, but 2 or more feet. Have her use the ruler or strip of cardboard and the yard stick to find the out how many feet are in a yard.

Have your student find a body part to use as reference for a yard and a foot in order to have some length in mind when making estimates. They can use the same reference they found for a meter, since a yard is about a meter. A foot may be about two hand spans.

Learning Tasks 1-4, US› pp. 59-60

4. **String B**

    1 yard = **3** feet

➤ Have your student estimate some additional lengths to the nearest yard or foot, and then measure to the nearest yard or foot.

US> Part 4 – Measuring Length in Inches

(42) Inches (US› pp. 61-62)

> ➢ Understand the inch as a unit of measurement.
> ➢ Estimate and measure lengths to the nearest inch.
> ➢ Add and subtract lengths in inches.
> ➢ Compare an inch with a foot.
> ➢ Compare an inch with a centimeter.

➤ Tell your student that in the US we measure things smaller than a foot in inches. Show her an inch on a **ruler**.

Page US› 61
Learning Task 1, US› p. 61

➤ Have your student estimate the lengths of some objects in inches and then measure. Since students learned about halves in Primary Mathematics 1B, you may want to her where the half-mark is on the ruler and have her measure objects to the nearest half inch. For example, the length of the object can be "about two and a half inches."

Have your student practice drawing lines of various lengths in inches.

Challenge your student to draw lines of a certain length, such as 4 inches, without a ruler, using a straight-edge without markings, such as a piece of cardboard. Then have him measure and see how close he came.

You can play the game *Guess the Length* suggested in the section on centimeters using inches instead.

US› Page 62
Tell you student that the drawings for the yard and meter are a scaled down. The ones for centimeter and inch are not. Your student can use two rulers and compare a centimeter to an inch.

US› Workbook Exercise 28

(43) Practice (US› p. 63, 3d› p. 59)

> ➤ Review addition and subtraction of 3-digit numbers.
> ➤ Solve word problems involving length.

Practice 3A

1. (a) **294**   (b) **399**   (c) **500**

2. (a) **571**   (b) **502**   (c) **960**

3. (a) **384**   (b) **187**   (c) **378**

4. (a) **129**   (b) **204**   (c) **319**

5. (a) **800**   (b) **178**   (c) **694**

6. Total distance = distance to post office + distance to library
   = 350 m + 550 m = **900 m**

7. Length of ribbon for bow = total length - remaining length
   = 90 cm - 35 cm = **55 cm**

US› 8. Total length = sum of length of each side

   = 24 yd + 12 yd + 16 yd + 12 yd = **64 yd**

3d› 8. Total length = sum of length of each side
   = 24 m + 12 m + 16 m + 12 m = **64 m**

US› 9. Nicole's height = Taylor's height – how much shorter Nicole is
   = 96 cm - 8 cm = **88 cm**

3d› 9. Meihua's height = Suling's height – how much shorter Meihua is
   = 96 cm - 8 cm – **88 cm**

(44) Review

> Review concepts learned so far in Primary Mathematics.

Workbook Review 2

Unit 4 – Weight

Part 1 – Measuring Weight in Kilograms

(45) Kilograms (US› pp. 64- 67, 3d› pp. 60-63)

➢ Understand the kilogram as a unit of measurement.
➢ Weigh objects to the nearest kilogram.
➢ Read scales in kilograms.
➢ Compare weights.
➢ Add and subtract weights in kilograms.

In *Primary Mathematics 1*, the student learned to compare weights by feel or "heft" and to measure weight in non-standard units. This section introduces the kilogram as the standard unit of weight. 1 kilogram is equal to the mass of the international platinum-iridium kilogram prototype kept under three glass bells in a safe (with three keys given to three different people) in the cellar of the Pavillion de Breteuil in Paris.

A kilogram is a measure of mass, not weight. We often use the terms "mass" and "weight" interchangeably in our daily speech, but to a scientist they are different things. The mass of a body is a measure of how much matter it contains. An object with mass has a quality called inertia. Mass is a measure of how much inertia an object displays, that is, how much force is needed to get it moving from a resting position or to stop it from moving once it is moving. Weight, in contrast, is a measure of the gravitational pull between two objects. A 1 kg mass on Earth would weigh less on the moon. Mass is measured by using a balance comparing a known mass to an unknown mass. Weight is measured on a scale. Kitchen scales calibrated in kilograms and grams are calibrated for use on Earth. The metric unit for weight is the Newton; on earth a mass of 1 kilogram weighs 9.8 Newtons. However, the US pound is a measure of weight, not mass. The slug is the English measurement of mass, and on earth a mass of one slug weighs 32.2 pounds.

Balances and metric weights are available at science supply stores. You can construct a simple balance using a small plywood board nailed to a can or by suspending cups from either side of a hanger or a ruler suspended from its middle. For small weights, a ruler can be balanced on a pencil. When comparing weights make sure the balance is centered, that is, the fulcrum is placed so that one side is balanced with the other side before adding any weights. You can adjust the balance of a board nailed to a can by adding some clay to one side or the other. You can adjust the balance made by suspending cups from a hangar by adjusting the distance of the string from the center. Simple commercial balances have a slider for centering the balance.

For reference, a liter (about a quart) of water weighs 1 kg. Post-1982 US pennies are about 2.5 g, so 400 pennies are about 1 kg.

US› In the US, your student may be more familiar with pounds as a unit of weight. 1 kg = 2.205 pounds. A good approximation is 1 kg = 2 pounds. A person weighing 30 kg weighs about 60 pounds.

Try to obtain a kilogram weight. You can measure out a kilogram bag of beans in the bulk food section of the grocery store and use that. Clay and play dough often come in weight amounts and can be used to make an amount close to 1 kg if from a new pack or can. For example, in the US you can buy 1 pound packages of modeling clay. Often they are divided into 4 sticks, each a quarter of a pound. 9 sticks are very close to 1 kilogram.

➤ Discuss with your student various ways in which weighing is used in everyday life. Ask her what types if things we weigh and why.

Use a simple **balance**. Let your student compare the weights of various objects. Ask him how we could tell another person the weight of something so that that person would know exactly how heavy it is without having it.

Tell your student that the kilogram is the standard unit of weight used in most countries. Give her a **kilogram weight** to hold. Have her compare the weight of various objects to a kilogram.

Ask your student: Which weighs more, a kilogram of tennis balls or a kilogram of rocks? (They both weigh the same.)

Use a zip lock bag and beans or rice and have your student make several kilogram weights using the weight you gave him and a balance.

Have your student estimate the weight of various objects (not more than abut 5 kg or however many weights he made) to the nearest kilogram and then weigh them.

➤ Draw two lines as shown below. Mark a point at the same place along both the lines and ask your student to name the point. Depending on the scale used, the point will represent a different number.

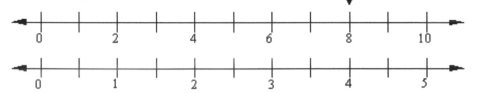

Practice reading scales or number lines with different divisions. Let your student read other scales around the house, such as a thermometer, a candy thermometer, a meat thermometer, the thermostat, the oven temperature, or scales at the store.

US> p. 64, 3d> p. 60
Learning Tasks 1-7, US> pp. 65-67, 3d> pp. 61-63
In learning task 6, you may need to point out that the two scales are different. In the first, a 6 kg weight will make the pointer go all the way around, whereas in the second, a 10 kg weight is needed. It takes more weight to "push the arrow around."

2.   (a) **2**   (b) **3**

3.   **Lighter**

4.   **More**

5.   **9**

6.   (a) A weighs 4 kg, B weighs 8 kg.
         6 kg - 4 kg = 2 kg. **B** is heavier by **2 kg**.
     (b) 4 kg +6 kg = 10 kg. The total weight is **10 kg**.

7.   (a) A weighs 1 kg. B weighs 4 kg. C weighs 5 kg. **C** is heaviest.
     (b) **A** is the lightest.
     (c) 1 kg + 4 kg + 5 kg = 10 kg. The total weight is **10 kg**.

Workbook Exercise 29

Part 2 – Measuring Weight in Grams

(46) Grams (US› pp. 68-69, 3d› pp. 64-65)

➢ Understand the gram as a unit of measurement.
➢ Estimate and weigh objects in grams.
➢ Add and subtract weight in grams.

In this section, the gram is introduced as a standard unit of weight for measuring the weight (or mass) of an object when it is less than a kilogram.

Two regular (small) paper clips weigh about 1 gram. One teaspoon of water weighs 5 grams. One US penny weighs about 2.5 grams.

If you have a balance, even a home-made one, and do not have commercially available weights, you can make some weights using combinations of pennies and paper clips (4 pennies weigh about 10 grams, 40 pennies weigh about 100 g). Put the 40 pennies in zip lock bags for a 100 g weight, tape 20 together for a 50 g weight, and tape 4 pennies together for a 10 g weight. You will need several of each.

➤ Tell your student that for objects weighing less than 1 kg we use grams. Use a **balance** and weights to measure the weight of objects that are less than 1 kg. If you have a gram weight, let him feel how heavy it is. Or tell him that two small paper clips or a unit block from a base-10 set weights about 1 g. Two pennies weigh about 5 g. If you don't have any weights, let him make some using pennies. Then have him weigh some objects. Note that a simple balance is not very accurate for small weights and depending on your balance it may be accurate only to about 10 g (that is, it is not possible to distinguish between 9 g an 10 g). If you can obtain a kitchen scale marked in grams, he can weigh objects using that. After weighing some objects, have him first guess the weight before weighing. You may want to tell him that there are 1000 grams in a kilogram.

Show your student cans of food and note the weight in grams. In the US, the weight will also be given in pounds and ounces.

US› p. 68, 3d p. 64
Learning Tasks 1-3, US› p. 69, 3d› p. 65

1.   (a) **400** g   (b) **600** g

2.   (a) **350** g   (b) **230** g

 Workbook Exercise 30

US› Part 3 – Measuring Weight in Pounds

---

(47) Pounds (US› pp. 70-71)

➢ Understand the pound as a unit of measurement.
➢ Estimate and weigh objects in pounds.
➢ Add and subtract weight in pounds.

The standard unit of weight in the US is the pound. A pound is about half as much as a kilogram (1 kg = 2.205 pounds). If your student is more familiar with pounds, when he sees a problem later in this math where the weight of a child is given, for example, as 30 kilograms, he might find it easier to picture the size of the child by doubling the weight to get 60 pounds as an approximate weight.

The abbreviation for pound is **lb** (from *libra*, the Latin word for a unit of weight).

Ask your student how much she weighs. Use a bathroom scale if you have one. Point out that in the US we use pounds as the common unit of weight. Find a **pound weight** (such as a commercially available weight, a can or some other food package that weighs a pound, like a pound of salt, a fishing weight, or a bag of beans weighed to a pound) and let her compare that to the **kilogram weight**.

If you have several pound weights, have your student weigh some objects using a balance. Have her try to guess the weight first.

Let your student weigh produce at the grocery store if it has scales.

 Learning Tasks 1-4, US› pp. 70-71

2. **heavier**

3. (a) the one **on the left**; **2 lb**
   (b) **16 lb**

US› Part 4 – Measuring Weight in Ounces

(48) Ounces, Practice (US› pp. 72-73)

> ➢ Understand the ounce as a unit of measurement.
> ➢ Estimate and weigh objects in ounces.
> ➢ Add and subtract weight in ounces.
> ➢ Review addition and subtraction of 3-digit numbers.
> ➢ Solve word problems involving weight or length.

The common unit of weight in the US for objects less than a pound is an ounce. There are 16 ounces in a pound. 1 ounce = 28.35 grams. 11 pennies or 5 quarters weigh about an ounce. Make some ounce weights for comparison to grams.

Tell your student that in the US the ounce is a standard unit of weight for objects less than a pound. Give her some ounce weights and let her compare them to grams. Use a balance or scale and let her guess and weigh some items in ounces.

Show your student some food items that are marked in both metric weight and standard weight.

Pages US› 72-73
Learning Tasks 1-2, US› p. 72

1.   **6, 10**

Practice 4A

1. (a) **261**   (b) **408**   (c) **533**
2. (a) **637**   (b) **856**   (c) **930**
3. (a) **193**   (b) **287**   (c) **320**
4. (a) **32**   (b) **480**   (c) **586**
5. (a) **554**   (b) **623**   (c) **535**

6. (a) The **durian** is heavier.
    (b) Grams heavier = the durian's weight - the papaya's weight
                      = 900 g - 550 g = **350 g**

7. (a) The father's weight = Raju's weight + how much heavier his father is
        = 39 kg + 28 kg = **67 kg**

    (b) The total weight = Raju's weight + the father's weight
        = 39 kg + 67 kg = **106 kg**

8. (a) The pear's weight = the mango's weight – grams lighter the pear is
        = 280 g - 60 g = **220 g**

    (b) Total weight = weight of mango + weight of pear
        = 280 g + 220 g = **500 g**

9. (a) Weight of pineapple = total weight - weight of apple
        = 840 g - 90 g = **750 g**

    (b) How much heavier = weight of pineapple - weight of apple
        = 750 g - 90 g = **660 g**

US›

Review the units of measurements learned so far. Tell your student that there are two systems of measurement. The metric system, which uses meters, centimeters, kilograms, and grams, is used in most countries. The US and a few other countries use yards, feet, inches, pounds, and ounces. This system of measurement is sometimes called the Imperial system, and is not used at the same time as the metric system. Things can be measured in yards and feet, or pounds and ounces, but are not measured in kilograms and ounces. In science, the metric system is used.

(49-50) Review (US> p. 75, 3d> p. 67)

 ➤ Review concepts learned so far in *Primary Mathematics*.

You can do the textbook review and/or the first workbook review to see if you need to review any concepts. Note that these are reviews and your student may need some reteaching or reminding of concepts; reviews don't mean the student is ready to be tested but can be used to see if material needs to be reviewed.

Review A

1. (a) **659**   (b) **715**   (c) **850**

2. (a) **977**   (b) **660**   (c) **1000**

3. (a) **402**   (b) **782**   (c) **810**

4. (a) **500**   (b) **350**   (c) **32**

5. (a) **184**   (b) **625**   (c) **398**

6. Length remaining = original length - length used
   = 20 m - 7 m = **13 m**

7. Total length used = sum of lengths used for each parcel
   = 96 cm + 85 cm = **181 cm**

8. Weight of papaya = total weight - weight of pear
   = 340 g - 95 g
   = **245 g**

9. (a) Weight of brother = weight of Sulin – kg lighter brother is
   = 34 kg - 8 kg = **26 kg**

   (b) Total weight = weight of Sulin + weight of brother
   = 34 kg + 26 kg = **60 kg**

 Workbook Review 3
Workbook Review 4

Unit 5 – Multiplication and Division

Part 1 – Multiplication

(51) Multiplication I (US› pp. 76-77, 3d› pp. 68-69)

> ➢ Understand multiplication as repeated addition.
> ➢ Write multiplication sentences.

Students were introduced to the concept of multiplication as repeated addition in *Primary Mathematics 1*. This is reviewed in this section. The emphasis in this section is on understanding multiplication, not on memorizing the multiplication facts. Allow your student to use manipulatives and repeated addition to solve the multiplication problems in this section.

Multiplication is associated with the part-whole concept. Given the number of equal parts and the number in each part, we can multiply to find the whole (the total).

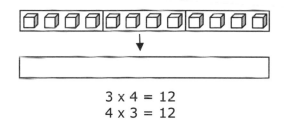

$$3 \times 4 = 12$$
$$4 \times 3 = 12$$

"3 groups of 4" can be written as 3 x 4 or 4 x 3. Do not teach your student that the first number has to be the number of groups. Students have learned in *Primary Mathematics 1* that 3 groups of 4 and 4 groups of 3 give the same answer, and that the order of the factors is not important. 4 x 3 could just as well be read as "4 each in 3 groups". By the time your student learns algebra, there will be no arbitrarily imposed order to the factors determined by which one is the number of parts and which one is the number in each parts.

Note that in task 1, there are 5 birds in 4 groups, 5 x 4. The number of groups is the second factor. In task 2, there are 5 groups of 6 hats, 5 x 6. The number of groups is the first factor.

➤ Place **objects** such as blocks, in groups, e.g. 3 groups of 5. Ask:

> How many groups are there?
> How many blocks are in each group?
> How can you find out how many blocks there are altogether?

To find the total number of blocks, we can add them together:
        5 + 5 + 5 = 15

This is quicker than simply counting the blocks one by one.

Multiplication means finding the total number of objects when you have equal groups.
Write the multiplication sentence 3 x 5 = 15. Tell your student that we use the multiplication symbol "x" in number sentences for multiplication.

3 x 5 means   5 + 5 + 5
                 3 groups of 5
                 3 fives
                 3 times 5
                 3 multiplied by 5
                 multiply 3 by 5
                 5 x 3

The student may write either 3 x 5 or 5 x 3. There are 3 groups of 5, or 5 in each of 3 groups.

US› p. 76, 3d› p. 68
Learning Tasks 1-3, US› pp. 76-77, 3d pp. 68-69

1. **20**   2. **30**

Workbook Exercise 31

(52) Multiplication II (US> pp. 78-79, 3d> pp. 70-71)

 ➢ Work out multiplication situations using repeated addition.

> Use objects around the house and ask questions such as:
> If there are 4 prongs on a fork, how many prongs are there on 5 forks?
> If a stool has 3 legs, how many legs are there on 6 stools?
> How many fingers are there on 4 hands?
> How many feet are there on 8 birds?

Give your student 5 counters and write "5 x 3". You can make up a story about a duplicating machine that multiplies what you put in by the amount you set the dial to. Have your student multiply the 5 counters by 3 by getting 2 more groups of 5.

Repeat with other multiplication expressions. You can write the first factor, and then have your student decide what he wants to set the dial on the duplicating machine to, and write the rest of the equation.

 Learning Task 3, US> p. 78, 3d> p. 70

3. (a) **21**   (b) **36**

 Workbook Exercises 32-33

(53) Arrays (US› p. 78, 3d› p. 70)

➢ Use rectangular arrays to illustrate multiplication.
➢ Write two related equations for a multiplication situation.

Arrange objects, such as pennies, blocks, or counters, in a rectangular array.
Ask:

How many rows are there? (3)
How many [blocks] are in each row? (4)
How many [blocks] are there altogether? (12)
What addition equation can we write to show this?
$4 + 4 + 4 = 12$

How many columns are there? (4)
How many [blocks] are there in each column? (3)
How many [blocks] are there altogether? (12)
What addition equation can we write to show this?
$3 + 3 + 3 + 3 = 12$

The arrangement of blocks can be thought of as 3 groups of 4 or 4 groups of 3.

What two multiplication equations can we write?
$4 \times 3 = 12$
$3 \times 4 = 12$

Write the expression 2 x 8 and have your student form the array. Ask her to decide which repeated addition is easiest,
$2 + 2 + 2 + 2 + 2 + 2 + 2 + 2$ or $8 + 8$.

Give your student 24 blocks and have him arrange them in different ways and write two equations for each.

Learning Task 4, p. 70

4.   (a) $4 \times 2 = \mathbf{8}$ (b) $5 \times 3 = \mathbf{15}$
          $2 \times 4 = \mathbf{8}$ $3 \times 5 = \mathbf{15}$

Workbook Exercise 34

(54) Practice (US› p. 79, 3d› p. 71)

 ➤ Practice multiplication concepts.

Practice 5A

1. 6 x 4 = **24** or 4 x 6 = 24
2. 2 x 5 = **10** or 5 x 2 =10
4. **6 x 3 = 18**; **3 x 6 = 18**
5. **3 x 5 = 15**; **5 x 3 = 15**

Ask your student to write one equation for problems 1 and 2, and two equations for problems 4 and 5.

X's

Material: **Number cubes**, paper and pencil

Single player: Roll the number cubes twice. After the first roll, draw the corresponding number of circles. After the second roll, draw X's in each circle. Write the multiplication sentence for the total number of X's. For example, a 4 and a 5 are rolled. 4 x 5 = 20

Multi-player: Take turns rolling twice. The player with the most stars wins.

Draw the Rectangle
Material: **Number cube 1-6, graph paper**

Single player: Roll the number cube. Draw a line on graph paper the length of squares equal to the number rolled. Roll again. Draw the height. Shade in squares to make a rectangle and write the multiplication sentences. For example, a 6 and 3 are rolled. 6 x 3 = 18 and 3 x 6 = 18. You can label the number cube with higher numbers, such as 5-10, or use two number cubes, labeled with different numbers.

Multi-player: Players take turns rolling the number cubes twice. The number of squares in the rectangle is the score. Each player rolls a specified number of times and the scores are added. The player with the highest score wins.

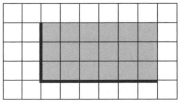

Part 2 – Division

The emphasis in this section is on understanding the meaning of division rather than on memorization of division facts or on finding division facts from multiplication facts. All the problems in this section have pictures. Allow your student to use manipulatives

Page 72 in the textbook illustrates two kinds of division situations:

> Sharing:
> > Start with a set of objects (12 balloons).
> > Make a given number of equal groups (3 groups).
> > Count the number of objects in each group (4 balloons).
> Grouping:
> > Start with a set of objects (12 balloons)
> > Make equal groups of a given size (4 balloons)
> > Count the number of groups made (3 groups).

Previously, students learned that addition and subtraction are associated with the part-whole concept. If we are given two parts, we can add to find the whole. If we are given the whole and a part, we can subtract to find the other part.

Multiplication and division are also associated with the part-whole concept. Instead of two different parts making a whole, a specified number of equal parts make the whole.

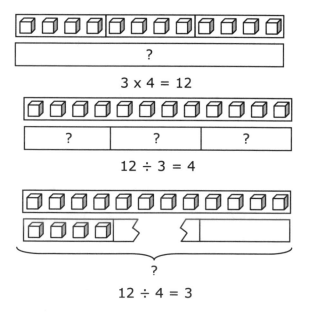

Given the number of equal parts and the number in each part, we can multiply to find the whole (total).

$$3 \times 4 = 12$$

Given the whole and the number of parts, we can divide to find the number in each part (sharing).

$$12 \div 3 = 4$$

Given the whole and the number in each part, we can divide to find the number of parts (grouping).

In *Primary Mathematics 3*, students will be introduced to the term "unit" for the equal parts. At this level, they should understand that both multiplication and division are associated with equal parts.

$$12 \div 4 = 3$$

(55) Sharing (US> pp. 80-82, 3d> pp. 72-74)

-☼- ➢ Understand division as sharing equally into a given number of groups.
➢ Use the division symbol (÷) to write division equations for sharing.
➢ Solve division problems with pictures.

The division symbol (÷) to write division sentences is new here, and was not taught in *Primary Mathematics 1*.

➤ Use 3 bowls or plates. Give your student 12 **objects**. Ask her to put an equal number of objects in each bowl. One way to do this is to first put one in each bowl, then a second in each bowl, then a third, and then a fourth. Ask her how many are in each group. Tell her we are dividing the objects up into 3 equal groups.

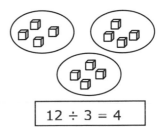

$$12 ÷ 3 = 4$$

Tell her we use the division symbol (÷) to show that we are dividing.
Write the division sentence 12 ÷ 3 = 4
Tell her 12 ÷ 3 means: 12 divided by 3
　　　　　　　　Divide 12 into 3 equal groups

Have her also arrange the 12 objects into 4 equal groups and write 12 ÷ 4 = 3.

Make sure your student understands the meaning of each of the operation symbols. Write some expressions such as the following and have him illustrate them with objects.
　　　8 + 2　　　8 – 2　　　8 x 2　　　8 ÷ 2

 Learning Tasks 1-3, US> pp. 81-82, 3d> pp. 73-74)

2. **5; 5**　　　3. **6; 6**

➤ Ask questions about division situations and write the division sentence. Use examples where the number of groups is given, and the student must determine how many go in each group. Let her use uniform **objects** such as counters or unit blocks to find the answer and write the equation. For example:
- If I have 15 cookies, how many would I give you and two friends so that you each had the same number of cookies? 15 ÷ 3 = 5
- Let's say you drank 14 cups of milk in a week. If you drank the same number of cups each day, how many cups did you drink each day? 14 ÷ 7 = 2

 Workbook Exercises 35-36

(56) Grouping (US> pp 83-84, 3d> pp. 75-76)

 ➢ Understand division as dividing a set of objects into groups of equal size.
➢ Write division equations for grouping.

 Give your student 12 **objects** and ask him to put them into groups of 4. He must first put 4 into a group, then 4 into another group, and then 4 into a third group. Ask how many groups there are.

Write the division sentence 12 ÷ 4 = 3
Tell him 12 ÷ 4 means: 12 divided by 4
                        Divide 12 into groups of 4

Point out that the answer is the same in 12 ÷ 4 = 3 whether it means "12 divided into groups of 4 gives 3 groups" or "12 divided into 4 equal groups gives 3 in each group".

Also have your student put the 12 objects into groups of 3 and write the division sentence 12 ÷ 3 = 4.

Division means to find either the number of equal groups or parts or the number of objects in each group or part.

Learning Tasks 4-6, US> pp. 83-84, 3d> pp. 75-76

5.   **5; 5**

6.   **6; 6**

 Ask some questions based on division situations. Use examples where the number that goes in each group is given, and the student must determine how many groups are needed. Let him use uniform **objects** such as counters or unit blocks to find the answer. Write the equation. For example:
    You have 16 cookies. You want to put 4 cookies on each plate. How many plates do you need? 16 ÷ 4 = 4
    You see 12 feet under the bottom of a curtain. How many people are behind the curtain? 12 ÷ 2 = 6

Workbook Exercises 37-38

(57) Multiplication and Division Sentences (US> p. 85, 3d> p. 77)

 ➤ Write two multiplication and two division sentences for a given set of equal groups or a rectangular array.

➤ Arrange some objects into equal groups.
Help your student write two multiplication and two division sentences.

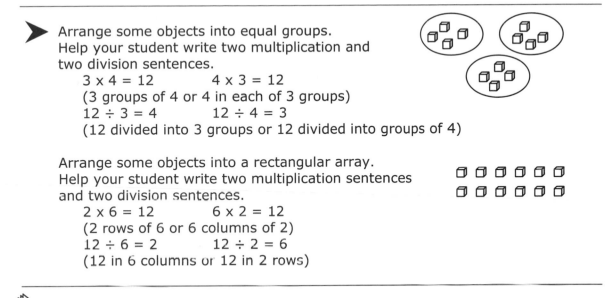

    3 x 4 = 12   4 x 3 = 12
    (3 groups of 4 or 4 in each of 3 groups)
    12 ÷ 3 = 4   12 ÷ 4 = 3
    (12 divided into 3 groups or 12 divided into groups of 4)

Arrange some objects into a rectangular array.
Help your student write two multiplication sentences and two division sentences.
    2 x 6 = 12   6 x 2 = 12
    (2 rows of 6 or 6 columns of 2)
    12 ÷ 6 = 2   12 ÷ 2 = 6
    (12 in 6 columns or 12 in 2 rows)

Learning Tasks 7-8, US> p. 85, 3d> p. 77

7.   **18; 18; 9; 2**

8.   **32; 32; 8; 4**

Workbook Exercise 39

(58) Practice (US> p. 86-87, 3d> pp. 78-79)

➢ Review multiplication and division concepts.
➢ Solve problems involving multiplication and division using pictures.

➤ Optional investigation:

Give your student 24 cubes or other objects. Have her arrange them into as many different groups as she can. She can put them in arrays. Have her write the division sentences:

$$24 \div 2 = 12$$
$$24 \div 3 = 8$$
$$24 \div 4 = 6$$
$$24 \div 6 = 4$$
$$24 \div 8 = 3$$
$$24 \div 12 = 2$$

Repeat with different numbers of objects. You can include prime numbers such as 13. When she realizes she can't group them, you can tell her it is a special number called a prime number. You can let her try other numbers to see if she can discover any other prime numbers.

Practice 5B
Ask your student to write the equations for these.

1. $12 \div 2 = \mathbf{6}$

2. $24 \div 6 = \mathbf{4}$

3. $30 \div 3 = \mathbf{10}$

4. $28 \div 4 = \mathbf{7}$

Practice 5C
Ask your student to write the equations for these.

1. $7 \times 3 = \mathbf{21}$ $3 \times 7 = \mathbf{21}$
   $21 \div 3 = \mathbf{7}$ $21 \div 7 = \mathbf{3}$

2. $18 \div 6 = \mathbf{3}$

3. $5 \times 4 = \mathbf{20}$

4. $35 \div 5 = \mathbf{7}$

(59) Review

 ➢ Review concepts learned so far in *Primary Mathematics*.

Workbook Review 5

Unit 6 – Multiplication Tables of 2 and 3

Part 1 – Multiplication Table of 2

---

(60) Counting by Twos (US› pp. 88-90, 3d› pp. 80-82)

➢ Count by twos.
➢ Relate counting by twos to 2 x ____ = _____

In this section, students will begin to study and commit multiplication facts to memory. By the end of this unit, students should know most of the facts for 2 and 3, both multiplication and division, or be able to quickly calculate the ones they haven't memorized.

Here, they will learn the multiplication facts for 2 through 2 x 10.

US› You may wish to include 2 x 11 and 2 x 12, since students in the U.S. will encounter twelves frequently. However, multiplication of a 2-digit number by a 1-digit number (e.g. 12 x 2) will be covered in *Primary Mathematics 3*, and the guide will give suggestions for learning how to do multiplication by a single digit mentally.

In this curriculum, even and odd numbers are taught along with division with a remainder in *Primary Mathematics 3*.

 Use **multilink cubes** or other objects joined in twos and teach your student to count them by twos to 20.

Use a **hundred chart**. Have your student circle the numbers he gets when counting by twos up to 10. Discuss with your student any patterns he may see. All of the numbers end in 2, 4, 6, 8, or 0. Cover up just the circled numbers up to 20. Have your student supply the covered numbers. Repeat until he can do it fairly quickly, both forwards and backwards.

Have your student practice counting by twos both forwards and backwards without the chart. He should continue practicing during later lessons until he can do it easily. Let your student hold up a finger for each two, first on one hand, then the next. Until he has the facts memorized, he can count by twos until he gets to the correct number of fingers. For example, for 2 x 7 he counts by twos until he has all five fingers of one hand and two of the other up.

Students should recognize if a number is in the twos sequence or not. Give your student a number between 1 and 20 and have him tell you if it is one of the numbers gotten when counting by twos.

Use objects such as **multilink cubes**. Set out 4 sets of 2. Write 2 + 2 + 2 + 2 = _____ and 2 x 4 = _____ and have your student supply the answer. Allow him to use repeated addition and holding up his fingers to arrive at the answer. Repeat with other sets of two up to 10 sets. Have your student write the equations.

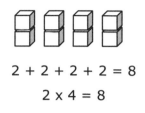

$$2 + 2 + 2 + 2 = 8$$

$$2 \times 4 = 8$$

 US› pp. 88-89, 3d› pp. 80-81
Learning Task 1, US› p. 90, 3d› p. 82

    (a) **6; 6**   (b) **14; 14**

1. (a) **4**   (b) **18**

 Workbook Exercises 40-41

(61) Multiplication Table of 2 (US› pp. 90-91, 3d› pp. 82-83)

 ➢ Build the multiplication table for 2.

➤ Lay out a two-unit **multilink cubes**. Have your student write the multiplication sentence for it next to it, making a chart. Continue adding a two-unit and writing the multiplication sentence. Stress the idea that the next one is "2 more." Continue to 2 x 10 = 20.

Starting with 2 x 10 and 10 sets of two-units, remove a two-unit one at a time and have your student say the multiplication equation at each step. Stress the idea that the next one is "2 less".

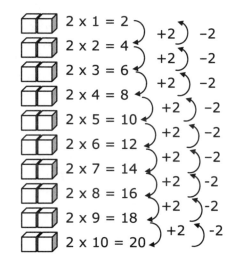

Have your student read or "chant" the chart periodically during the next few lessons - "two times one is two, two times two is four …", or "two one two, two two four, … ." Then have him say the multiplication facts of two without the chart.

By now your student may know some of the multiplication facts of 2. He can determine the ones he does not know by either adding 2 or subtracting 2 from the ones he knows.

 Learning Tasks 2-4, US› pp. 90-91, 3d› pp. 82-83

2. (a) **6**   (b) **8**

3. **12**

4. **8**; **10**; **12**; **14**; **16**; **18**; **20**

 Workbook Exercises 42-43

(62) Related Facts (US› pp. 91-92, 3d› pp. 83-84)

- ➤ Relate multiplication by 2 to doubling in addition.
- ➤ Relate the associated facts 2 x _____ and _____ x 2.

➤ Put sets of 2 **multilink cubes** in a rectangular array. Show that the array can be divided into either rows or columns, and that the array can be represented by:
$$2 + 2 + 2 + 2 + 2 = 2 \times 5$$
$$5 + 5 = 5 \times 2$$
Point out that if she knows 2 x 5, then she also knows 5 x 2.

Write the numbers 2, 4, 6, 8, 10, 12, 14, 16, 18, and 20 on index cards. Shuffle, then have your student draw one at a time, and write or say two facts for each. For example, she draws 12 and writes or says 2 x 6 and 6 x 2.

Learning Tasks 5-8, US› pp. 91-92, 3d› pp. 83-84

5. (a) **10**; **10**   (b) **14**; **14**

6. (a) **16**; **16**   (b) **18**; **18**

7. (a) **8**; **10**; **12**; **14**; **16**; **18**; **20**

8. **6**; **2**; **9**

➤ Challenge your student with this problem, which involves doubling:
In 2 days, 2 chickens lay 5 eggs. If this is true for all chickens, how many eggs will 4 chickens lay in 4 days. (20)

Your student can create a table, doubling first the days, which doubles the eggs, and then the chickens, which also doubles the eggs.

days	chickens	eggs
2	2	5
4	2	10
4	4	20

 Workbook Exercise 44

(63) Multiplication Facts for 2

➢ Work on memorizing the multiplication facts for 2.

Help your student memorize the multiplication facts for 2. The following activities can be used now and/or later.

- Use Mental Math 23-25 in the appendix over the next few days. Show your student how to fill in the multiplication tables. Mental Math 25 can be done orally.

- Make a set of **fact cards** for the multiplication facts with the answers on the back. Shuffle and show your student each card. If he gives the correct answer, put it in his pile; if he gives the wrong answer, tell him the correct answer and put the card in your pile. Repeat with your pile until he has all the cards. If your student can handle timed drills, show him the card for a certain number of seconds (which you count silently). If he gets the answer correct within the time limit, he gets the card; if not, tell him the answer and keep the card. Repeat until he has all the cards. In subsequent practices, reduce the time limit. Either mix the order (some with 2 x _____ and some with _____ x 2) or include both.

- Use a set of **playing cards** without the face cards. Ace is one. Shuffle and place the cards face down. Draw one at card at a time and have your student supply the fact for 2 times the number drawn. If correct, place the cards in one pile; if wrong, place them in a second pile. Repeat with the second pile.

- Play Concentration. Write the following on **index cards**: 2 x 1, 2 x 2, 2 x 3, 2 x 4, 2 x 5, 2 x 6, 2 x 7, 2 x 8, 2 x 9, 2 x 10. Write the answers on another set of cards: 2, 4, 6, 8, 10, 12, 14, 16, 18, 20. Choose 5 multiplication cards and 5 corresponding answer cards. Mix them up and lay them face down in a 5 x 4 array. Your student turns up two at a time. If they match, he removes them. If not, he turns them face down. Repeat with another two. Continue until all have been removed. Repeat with the other 5 facts. Choose more pairs and make the array larger.

 Workbook Exercise 45

(64) Word Problems (US› pp. 92-93, 3d pp. 84-85)

 ➢ Solve word problems involving multiplication by 2.

 Practice 6A, #1-5, US› p. 93, 3d› p. 85
You can have your student supply the answers orally as part of a lesson.

1. (a) **6**   (b) **8**   (c) **4**
2. (a) **2**   (b) **18**   (c) **16**
3. (a) **12**   (b) **14**   (c) **20**
4. (a) **10**   (b) **6**   (c) **8**
5. (a) **18**   (b) **12**   (c) **14**

➤ Give your student some word problems where multiplication by 2 is used. By now, he should have the facts mostly memorized, and should be able to answer without using manipulatives. For example:

How many wheels do 8 bikes have? (8 x 2 = 16)
I have 2 bags each weighing 7 kg. How much do they weigh altogether? (2 x 7 = 14)

Learning Task 9, US p. 92, 3d› p. 84

9.   12; 12

Practice 6A, #6-10, US› p. 93, 3d› p. 85
Discuss these problems with your student. Ask your student what are the equal parts, how many equal parts there are, and how much is in each part. For example, for #6, there are 6 birds, so there are 6 equal parts, and there are 2 wings in each part. To find the total number of wings, we multiply the number of equal parts by the number of parts, or 6 x 2. You can allow your student to model the problem with objects, if necessary. You can show a model like the ones below, showing equal parts and the total, similar to the model for part-part whole in addition, except that there can be more than two parts and all the parts are the same. Do not require your student to draw these kinds of models yet. Your student may write the related multiplication equation instead (e.g. 2 x 6 = 12 for #6 instead of 6 x 2 = 12).

6.   6 x 2 = 12

     12 wings

bird	bird	bird	bird	bird	bird
2 wings	2 wings	2 wings	2 wings	2 wings	2 wings
total cost ?					

7.   10 x 2 = 20

   20 balloons

child 2	child 2	child 2	child 2	child 2	child 2	child 2	child 2	child 2	child 2
total balloons ?									

8.   2 x 5 = 10

   $10

week $5	week $5
total money ?	

9.   4 x 2 = 8

   8 kg

packet 2 kg	packet 2 kg	packet 2 kg	packet 2 kg
total weight ?			

10. 2 x 8 = 16

   16 m

curtain 8 m	curtain 8 m
total length ?	

 Make a game board with multiples of 2 in random order. Make the spaces large enough to hold your number cards.

2	16	4	6	2
14	10	4	12	6
8	14	18	20	10
20	12	18	8	16

Give your student 2 sets of cards 1-9 shuffled. Have her draw one at a time and lay the card on the multiple of 2. You can time her and let her see if she can beat her previous time.

📖✏️ **Workbook Exercise 46**

Part 2 – Multiplication Table of 3

(65) Counting by Threes (US> pp. 94-95, 3d> pp. 86-87)

➤ Count by threes.
➤ Relate counting by threes to 3 x ___ = _____.

Use **multilink cubes** or other objects joined in threes and teach your student to count them by threes to 30. Practice counting by threes both forward and backward.

Use a **hundred chart** and **coins or counters**. Cover up all the threes up to 30. Have your student supply the covered numbers.

Have your student practice counting by threes both forwards and backwards without the chart. Until he has the facts memorized, he can use his fingers to keep track of how many threes he has counted.

Use objects such as **multilink cubes**. Set out 4 sets of 3 objects. Write 3 x 4 = _____ and have your student supply the answer. Allow him to use repeated addition and to hold up his fingers to arrive at the answer. Repeat with other examples.

 US> pp. 94-95, 3d> pp. 86-87
Learning Task 1, US> p. 95, 3d> p. 87

(a) **15; 15**   (b) **27; 27**

1. (a) **12**   (b) **24**

Workbook Exercises 47-48

(66) Related Facts (US› p. 96, 3d› p. 88)

Relate the associated facts 3 x _____ and _____ x 3.

> Put sets of 3 **multilink cubes** in a rectangular array. Show that the array can be divided into either rows or columns, and that the array can be represented by:

$$3 + 3 + 3 + 3 + 3 = 3 \times 5$$
$$5 + 5 + 5 = 5 \times 3$$

Tell the student that if she knows 3 x 5, then she also knows 5 x 3.

Write the multiples of 3 from 3 to 30 on index cards. Shuffle, then have your student draw one at a time, and write or say two facts for each. For example, she draws 12 and writes or says 3 x 4 and 4 x 3. Let her count by 3 and use her fingers if necessary.

 Learning Tasks 3-4, US› p.96, 3d› p. 88

2.   **18**; **18**

3.   **2**; **3**; **8**

 Workbook Exercise 49

(67) Multiplication Table of 3 (US› pp. 96-97, US› pp. 88-89)

 ➤ Build the multiplication table for 3.

➤ Lay out a three-unit **multilink cubes**. Have your student write the multiplication sentence for it next to it, making a chart. Continue adding a three-unit and writing the multiplication sentence. Stress the idea that the next one is "3 more." Continue to 3 x 10 = 20.

Starting with 3 x 10 and 10 sets of three-units, remove a three-unit one at a time and have yours student say the multiplication equation at each step. Stress the idea that the next one is "3 less".

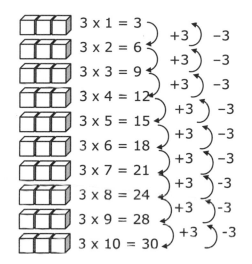

By now your student may know some of the multiplication facts of 3. He can calculate the ones he does not know by either adding 3 or subtracting 3 from the ones he knows.

 Learning Tasks 4-6, US› pp. 96-97, 3d› pp. 88-89

4. **12; 15; 18; 21; 24; 27; 30**
   3; 6; 9; 12; 15; 18; 21; 24; 27; 30

5. **18**

6. **24**

📖 **Workbook Exercises 50-52**

(68) Multiplication Facts for 3 (US› p. 98, 3d› p. 90)

 ➤ Work on memorizing the multiplication facts for 3.

 Help your student memorize the multiplication facts of 3. Adapt some of the activities and games given for practicing multiplication facts for 2. You can add in the facts for 2 as well. Do the practices or games at other times as you go on to new topics as necessary.

Use Mental Math 26-28 in the appendix over the next few days. Show your student how to fill in the multiplication tables. Mental Math 25 can be done orally.

➤ Use **playing cards** with face cards removed or four sets of number cards 1-10 and a **coin** or **counter**. Put a sticker with a 2 on it on one side of the coin, and a sticker with 3 on it on the other side of the coin. Shuffle the cards. Show one at a time as your student throws the coin. If he throws 2, he gives the multiple of 2 for the number on the card; if he throws a 3, he gives the multiple of 3. He gets the card if he is correct; if he is wrong, put the card at the bottom of the deck. Continue until he has all the cards.

 Practice 6B, #1-5, US› p. 98, 3d› p. 90
You can have your student supply the answers orally as part of a lesson.

1. (a) **3**   (b) **6**   (c) **12**
2. (a) **18**   (b) **21**   (c) **24**
3. (a) **12**   (b) **15**   (c) **30**
4. (a) **21**   (b) **27**   (c) **9**
5. (a) **24**   (b) **30**   (c) **18**

 Workbook Exercise 53

(69) Word Problems (US pp. 97-98, 3d› pp. 89-90)

 ➤ Solve word problems involving multiplication by 3.

Give your student some word problems where multiplication by 3 is used. By now, he should have the facts memorized, and should be able to answer without using manipulatives. Explain to him that in these problems he is being given a number of equal parts and the number in each part, so he needs to multiply to find the whole. You can ask him for the part, and the number in each part. For example:

How many wheels do 8 tricycles have? (8 x 3 = 24)
There are 3 buildings each with 7 apartments. How many apartments altogether? (3 x 7 = 21)
3 buses with a length of 8 m each are parked in a row. There is a gap of 2 m between each bus. What is the distance between the front of the first bus and the end of the last bus in the row? (Draw a picture.
buses: 3 x 8 = 24 gaps: 2 x 2 = 4   total: 24 + 4 = 28 m)

 Learning Task 7 (US› p. 97, 3d› p. 89)
There are 7 equal parts, the packets of sugar. The amount in each part is the weight, 3 kg.

7.   **21; 21**

Practice 6B, #6-10, US› p. 98, 3d› p. 90
Discuss these problems with your student. Ask your student what are the equal parts, how many equal parts there are, and how much is in each part.

6.   4 tricycles, each with 3 wheels.
     Total wheels = 4 x 3 = **12**

7.   3 rows, each with 7 trees.
     Total trees = 3 x 7 = **21**

8.   3 bag, each weighing 8 kg.
     Total weight = 3 x 8 kg = **24 kg**

US› 9.   6 dresses, each with 3 yd of cloth
     Total length = 6 x 3 yd = **18 yd**

3d› 9.   6 dresses, each with 3 m of cloth
     Total length = 6 x 3 m = **18 m**

10. 3 sets, each with 10 stamps
     Total stamps = 3 x 10 = **30**

 Workbook Exercise 54

(70) Practice (US p. 99, 3d› p. 91)

➤ Practice multiplication by 2 and 3.

➤ Continue practicing the multiplication facts for 2 and 3, using games or other practice such as the mental math. You may want to spend several days on this.

 Practice 6C

1. (a) **2**   (b) **3**   (c) **8**
2. (a) **10**   (b) **12**   (c) **18**
3. (a) **16**   (b) **27**   (c) **9**
4. (a) **20**   (b) **24**   (c) **21**
5. (a) **14**   (b) **15**   (c) **18**
6. Total books = number of weeks x books read each week = 5 x 3 = **15**
7. Total cost = number of tickets x cost for each ticket = 2 x 7 = **$14**
8. Total legs = number of bees x number of legs on each bee = 3 x 6 = **18**
9. Total length = number of pillowcases x length for each pillowcase = 9 x 2
                                                                    = **18 m**
10. Total weight = number of bags x weight for each bag = 3 x 10
                                                        = **30 US› lb, 3d› kg**

➤ Your student should begin to recognize numbers as belonging to the pattern of counting by 2 or by 3 (multiples of 2 or 3). Draw the following:

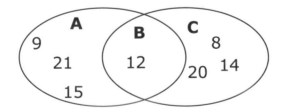

Ask her whether to put the number 6 in region A, B, or C. Help her see that numbers in the counting pattern of 3 are in region A, numbers in the counting pattern of 2 are in region C, and numbers in both counting patterns are in region B. So 6 would be in B. Ask her where to put the following numbers:
27   (A)   4   (C)
24   (B)   16   (C)
18   (B)

Three in a Row

Material: Multiplication by 2 and 3 game board (in appendix), **counters** (a different color for each player) **playing cards** with face cards removed, a **coin** with x2 on one side and x3 on the other or a **number cube** labeled with x2 or x3 only.

Procedure: Players take turns drawing a card and throwing the number cube or flipping the coin. They multiply the numbers together and place their counter on a square on the game board with the answer. The first student to get three counters in a row wins.

Workbook Exercise 55

Part 3 – Dividing by 2

(71) Division by 2 (US> pp. 100-101, 3d> pp. 92-93)

➢ Relate division facts to multiplication facts for 2.
➢ Divide by 2.

In this section, your student will relate multiplication facts for 2 to division by 2 and use the relationship to solve division problems. For example, if given the division problem $18 \div 2 = ?$, he can think of $? \times 2 = 18$ and recall the appropriate multiplication fact. He should eventually memorize the division facts through adequate practice provided by you in the form of games, drill sheets, computer software, etc.

➤ Put blocks or other objects in 2 groups.
Ask:

How many blocks are in each group? (4)
How many groups are there? (2)
How many blocks are there altogether? (8)

Write:

$$4 \xrightarrow{\times 2} 8 \qquad 4 \times 2 = 8$$

Ask:

If we start with 8 blocks and put them in 2 groups, how many would be in each group? (4)

Write:

$$4 \underset{\div 2}{\overset{\times 2}{\rightleftarrows}} 8 \qquad \begin{aligned} 4 \times 2 &= 8 \\ 8 \div 2 &= 4 \end{aligned}$$

Explain that to find 8 divided by 2, think of a number multiplied by 2 to give 8.

Write the problems shown at the right, one at a time, first the multiplication problem, followed by the corresponding division problem, and have your student supply the missing number.

____ x 2 = 2   2 ÷ 2 = ____

____ x 2 = 4   4 ÷ 2 = ____

____ x 2 = 6   6 ÷ 2 = ____

____ x 2 = 8   8 ÷ 2 = ____

____ x 2 = 10   10 ÷ 2 = ____

____ x 2 = 12   12 ÷ 2 = ____

____ x 2 = 14   14 ÷ 2 = ____

____ x 2 = 16   16 ÷ 2 = ____

____ x 2 = 18   18 ÷ 2 = ____

____ x 2 = 20   20 ÷ 2 = ____

US› p. 100, 3d› p. 92
Learning Tasks 1-2, US› p. 101, 3d› p. 93

3; 5

1.   (a) **4**   (b) **7**

2.   **8; 8**   **10; 10**

➤   Help your student memorize the division facts for 2. Use fact cards, games, or other activities adapted from those given for the multiplication facts. You may also use Mental Math 29.

Workbook Exercise 56

---

(72) Word Problems (US› pp. 102-103, 3d pp. 94-95)

-🔆- ➢   Solve word problems involving division by 2.

▶ Discuss with your student what she has learned so far in solving word problems involving addition, subtraction, and multiplication. Demonstrate with objects and write equations as necessary. You can use **counters** and bowls, or other objects.

For addition, we are given two or more unequal parts (usually), and asked to find the total. For example, we have 4 red counters and 3 blue counters and want to find the total. We add: 3 + 4 = 7

For subtraction, we are given a total and one or more parts, and asked to find a final part. For example, we are told that there are 18 red and blue counters. This is the total. 12 of them are red. This is a part. To find the number of blue counters, we subtract: 18 – 12 = 7.

For multiplication, we are given the number of groups, or equal parts, the amount in each part, and asked to find the total. For example, there are 2 bowls, each with 8 counters. To find the total number of counters, we multiply: 8 x 2 = 16.

Multiplication is repeated addition, so for both addition and multiplication we are finding a total.

We can think of division as being repeated subtraction. When we group objects into equal parts, we are repeatedly taking away the same amount. So with word problems involving division, we are given a total. We are also given either the number of equal parts and want to find the amount that goes in each part (sharing), or we are given the amount that goes in each part and want to find the number of equal parts (grouping). For example, there are 8 counters. We want to find how many go into 2 bowls equally. We divide: 8 ÷ 2 = 4. Or, we want to find how many groups of 4 we can make. We divide: 8 ÷ 4 = 2.

In discussing the problems in the learning tasks, ask questions such as
> Do we have a total amount?
> What else are we given? (the number of groups or the number of parts)
> What must we find? (the number in each group or the number of groups)
> How do we find this? (We divide.)

Allow your student to use objects to act out the problems, if necessary.

📖 **Learning Tasks 3-6, US› pp. 102-103, 3d pp. 94-95**

3. **4; 4**   4. **7, 7**   5. **6; 6**   6. **9; 9**

 **Workbook Exercise 57**

(73) Practice (US› p. 104, 3d› p. 96)

- ➢ Practice multiplication by 2 and 3 and division by 2.

If your student is weak on word problems, you may want to do Practice 6D as a lesson. Some of the word problems involve multiplication and some involve division. Help your student see whether a total needs to be found, or if it is given. Let her act out the problems with objects, if necessary.

Your student should continue practicing the multiplication facts for 2 and 3 and division facts for 3 as needed.

Practice 6D

1. (a) **8**   (b) **10**   (c) **4**
2. (a) **4**   (b) **5**   (c) **2**
3. (a) **12**   (b) **18**   (c) **16**
4. (a) **6**   (b) **9**   (c) **8**
5. (a) **7**   (b) **1**   (c) **10**
6. 20 ÷ 2 = **10**
7. $18 ÷ 2 = **9**
8. 2 x $5 = **$10**
9. 16 m ÷ 2 = **8 m**
10. 14 ÷ 2 = **7**

Part 4 – Dividing by 3

(74) Division by 3 (US› p. 105, 3d› p. 97)

➢ Relate division facts to multiplication facts.
➢ Divide by 3.

▶ From the previous section, your student should understand how division facts are related to multiplication facts. If necessary, you can review this. Put blocks or other **objects** in 3 groups.

Ask:

How many blocks are in each group? (4)
How many groups are there? (3)
How many blocks are there altogether? (12)

Write:

Ask:
$$4 \xrightarrow{\text{x 3}} 12 \qquad 4 \times 3 = 12$$

If we start with 12 blocks and put them in 3 groups, how many would be in each group?

Write:
$$4 \overset{\text{x 3}}{\underset{\div\, 3}{\rightleftarrows}} 12 \qquad \begin{array}{l} 4 \times 3 = 12 \\ 12 \div 3 = 4 \end{array}$$

Explain that, to find 12 divided by 3, think of a number multiplied by 3 to give 12.

▶ Write the problems at the right, one at a time, first the multiplication problem, followed by the corresponding division problem, and have your student supply the missing number.

___ x 3 = 3	3 ÷ 3 = ___
___ x 3 = 6	6 ÷ 3 = ___
___ x 3 = 9	9 ÷ 3 = ___
___ x 3 = 12	12 ÷ 3 = ___
___ x 3 = 15	15 ÷ 3 = ___
___ x 3 = 18	18 ÷ 3 = ___
___ x 3 = 21	21 ÷ 3 = ___
___ x 3 = 24	24 ÷ 3 = ___
___ x 3 = 27	27 ÷ 3 = ___
___ x 3 = 30	30 ÷ 3 = ___

Learning Task 1, US› p. 105, 3d› p. 97

1. **8; 8   5; 5**
    7; 7   9; 9

Workbook Exercise 58

(75) Division Facts for 3, Word Problems (US› p. 106, 3d› p. 98

> ➤ Work on memorizing the division facts for 3.
> ➤ Solve word problems involving division by 3.

Help your student memorize the division facts for 3. Use fact cards, games, or other activities adapted from those given for the multiplication facts.

Learning Tasks 2-3, p. 98

In each of these problems, your student should see that a whole is given, and either the number of groups or the number in each group. Allow your student to act it out with objects, if necessary.

2. **10**

3. **8**

Workbook Exercise 59

(76) Practice (US› pp. 107-108, 3d› pp. 99-100)

➢ Practice multiplication and division by 2 and 3.

Your student should continue practicing the multiplication and division facts for 2 and 3 as needed. Below are two more game suggestions. You can also use Mental Math 30, 31, and 32.

 Practice 6E

1. (a) **12**   (b) **18**   (c) **15**

2. (a) **4**   (b) **6**   (c) **5**

3. (a) **27**   (b) **21**   (c) **24**

4. (a) **9**   (b) **7**   (c) **8**

5. (a) **3**   (b) **2**   (c) **10**

6. Total bottles = 30.
   Number of parts or groups = 3 boxes
   We need to find the number of bottles in each box. We divide.
   30 ÷ 3 = 10   There are **10** bottles in each box.

7. Total spent = $18.
   Number of 1 kg parts = 3
   We need to find the amount of money for each kg. We divide.
   $18 ÷ 3 = $6   1 kg costs **$6**.

8. Total soldiers = 15.
   Number of rows (parts) = 3
   We need to find the number in each row. We divide.
   15 ÷ 3 = 5   There are **5** soldiers in each row.

9. Number of books = 9.
   Cost for each book = $3
   We need to find the total cost. We multiply.
   9 x $3 = $27   He paid **$27** altogether.

10. Total number of beads = 24.
    Number of strings (parts) = 3
    We need to find the number of beads on each string. We divide.
    24 ÷ 3 = 8   There are **8** beads on each string.

Three in a Row

Game 1 Material: Division by 2 and 3 **game board** (in appendix), **counters** (a different color for each player), two sets of cards (**index cards**) with the following expressions: 3 ÷ 3, 6 ÷ 3, 9 ÷ 3, 12 ÷ 3, 15 ÷ 3, 18 ÷ 3, 21 ÷ 3, 24 ÷ 3, 27 ÷ 3, 30 ÷ 3, 2 ÷ 2, 4 ÷ 2, 6 ÷ 2, 8 ÷ 2, 10 ÷ 2, 12 ÷ 2, 14 ÷ 2, 16 ÷ 2, 18 ÷ 2, 20 ÷ 2

Game 2 Material: Multiplication and Division by 2 and 3 **game board** (in appendix), **counters** (a different color for each player), one set of the cards listed for game 1 and 1 set of multiplication cards: 1 x 2, 2 x 2, 3 x 2, 4 x 2, 5 x 2, 6 x 2, 7 x 2, 8 x 2, 9 x 2, 10 x 2, 1 x 3, 2 x 3, 3 x 3, 4 x 3, 5 x 3, 6 x 3, 7 x 3, 8 x 3, 9 x 3, 10 x 3.

Procedure: Cards are shuffled and placed face down in the middle. Players take turns turning over a card and placing their markers on the squares with the answers. The first player to get three in a row vertically, horizontally, or diagonally wins.

Workbook Exercises 60-61

(77) Practice (US› pp. 107-108, 3d› pp. 99-100)

➤ Practice multiplication and division by 2 and 3.

Practice 6F

1. (a) **5**   (b) **7**   (c) **4**
2. (a) **3**   (b) **5**   (c) **4**
3. (a) **6**   (b) **8**   (c) **10**
4. (a) **6**   (b) **8**   (c) **7**
5. (a) **9**   (b) **10**   (c) **9**
6. 24 ÷ 3 = 8   **8 cm**
7. 30 ÷ 3 = 10   **10** weeks
8. 7 x 2 = 14   **$14**
9. 16 ÷ 2 = 8   **8** packets
10. 18 ÷ 3 = 6   **$6**

➤ **US› Enrichment - Measurement**

You can use standard measurement to practice word problems involving multiplication and division by 2 and 3. This topic will be covered more fully in *Primary Mathematics 3B*.

Show your student a **yardstick** and tell him that there are 3 feet in each yard.

Ask the following types of questions:

How many feet in 5 yards? (3 x 5 = 15)
(Here, a yard is a part containing 3 feet. 5 yards is the number of parts. We multiply.)

A piece of string is 1 yard long. How many feet in 8 strings of the same length? (3 x 8 = 24)

2 yd = _____ ft (6)
6 yd = _____ ft (18)

12 feet is how many yards?   (12 ÷ 3 = 4)
(Here, the yard is a part containing 3 feet. The total number of feet is given, so to find the number of parts, we divide.)

15 ft = _____ yd (3)
30 ft = _____ yd (10)

Use a pint container, a quart container, and a measuring cup. Show that there are 2 cups in a pint, and 2 pints in a quart.

Ask questions such as:

I want to make 3 cakes. Each cake needs a pint of milk.
How many pints do I need? (3 x 1 = 3)
How many cups to I need? (3 x 2 = 6)

We need 16 pints of juice for a party. The juice comes in quart containers.
How many quart containers do we need? (16 ÷ 2 = 8)

I have 10 pints of milk.
How many quarts is that? (10 ÷ 2 = 5)
How many cups is that? (10 x 2 = 20)

Workbook Exercises 62

(78-80) Review (US› pp. 109-112, 3d› pp. 101-104)

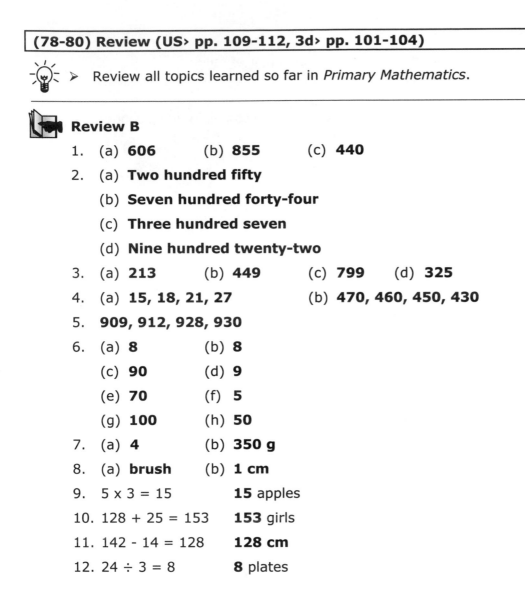

> Review all topics learned so far in *Primary Mathematics*.

Review B

1. (a) **606**   (b) **855**   (c) **440**

2. (a) **Two hundred fifty**
   (b) **Seven hundred forty-four**
   (c) **Three hundred seven**
   (d) **Nine hundred twenty-two**

3. (a) **213**   (b) **449**   (c) **799**   (d) **325**

4. (a) **15, 18, 21, 27**   (b) **470, 460, 450, 430**

5. **909, 912, 928, 930**

6. (a) **8**   (b) **8**
   (c) **90**   (d) **9**
   (e) **70**   (f) **5**
   (g) **100**   (h) **50**

7. (a) **4**   (b) **350 g**

8. (a) **brush**   (b) **1 cm**

9. 5 x 3 = 15   **15** apples

10. 128 + 25 = 153   **153** girls

11. 142 - 14 = 128   **128 cm**

12. 24 ÷ 3 = 8   **8** plates

Review C

1. (a) **408**   (b) **590**   (c) **555**

2. (a) **78**   (b) **703**   (c) **734**

3. (a) **18**   (b) **24**   (c) **16**

4. (a) **9**   (b) **8**   (c) **8**

5. (a) **7**   (b) **10**   (c) **10**

6. (a) **689**   (b) **505**
   (c) **40**   (d) **0**

7. (a) **<**   (b) **>**

    (c) **>**   (d) **<**

8. (a) **130**   (b) **120**

9. 128 + 94 + 46 = 268   **268** members

10. 120 - 89 = 31   **$31** more

11. 3 x 6 = 18   **18** cakes

12. 27 ÷ 3 = 9   **$9**

13. 820 + 95 = 915   **915** coconut trees

14. 145 + 65 = 210   **$210**

15. 18 ÷ 2 = 9   **9** shirts

 Workbook Review 6
Workbook Review 7

Answers and Solutions to Workbook Exercises

Exercise 1

1. (a) **37; 37; 37**   (b) **58; 58; 58**   (c) **94; 94; 94**

2. (a) **49**   (b) **62**   (c) **80**   (d) **100**

3. (a) 24 = **2** tens and **4** ones
    (b) 42 = **4** tens and **2** ones, **2** goes in the box
    (c) 67 = **6** tens and **7** ones, **67** goes in the box

4. (a) **49**   (b) **52**   (c) **66**   (d) **100**

5. (a) **46**   (b) **67**   (c) **58**

    (d) **93**   (e) **81**   (f) **25**

6. (a) **fifty**   (b) **sixty-four**   (c) **twenty-one**
    (d) **ninety-nine**   (e) **thirty-two**   (f) **one hundred**

Exercise 2

1. (a) **77**   (b) **75**   (c) **86**   (d) **66**

2. (a) **78**   (b) **74**   (c) **96**   (d) **56**

3. (a) **40**   (b) **73**   (c) **100**
    (d) **73**   (e) **76**   (f) **74**

4. (a) **56**   (b) **57**   (c) **65**   (d) **75**
    (e) **54**   (f) **53**   (g) **45**   (h) **35**

5. (a) **71**   (b) **72**   (c) **80**   (d) **90**
    (e) **69**   (f) **68**   (g) **60**   (h) **50**

6. (a) **49**   (b) **50**   (c) **58**   (d) **68**
    (e) **47**   (f) **46**   (g) **38**   (h) **28**

Exercise 3

1. (a) **50**   (b) **59**   (c) **28**   (d) **70**   (e) **87**   (f) **100**

2. (a) **45**   (b) **87**   (c) **63**   (d) **100**   (e) **70**   (f) **57**

3. (a) **23**   (b) **24**
    (c) **29**   (d) **78**   (e) **54**   (f) **87**   (g) **60**   (h) **98**

4. (a) **31**   (b) **50**   (c) **45**   (d) **56**   (e) **15**   (f) **36**

5. (a) **67, 76, 78, 87**   (b) **90, 82, 79, 66**

7. (a) **>**   (b) **<**   (c) **>**   (d) **<**   (e) **<**
    (f) **>**   (g) **>**   (h) **<**   (i) **<**   (j) **>**

Exercise 4

1. (a) **214**   (b) **346**   (c) **305**
   (d) **472**   (e) **563**   (f) **660**
   (g) **790**   (h) **307**

2. **129   219   355   535   553   740   704**

3. (a) **175**   (b) **253**   (c) **240**   (d) **407**

4. **611   309   293   390   90   6   500   60**

Exercise 5

1. (a) **460**   (b) **303**   (c) **339**

2. (a) **56**   (b) **325**   (c) **761**   (d) **430**   (e) **606**

Exercise 6

1. **320   440   541   792   404   514   729   958   985**

2. **109   207   320   411   515   1000   940   861**

3. **eight hundred four**   **four hundred forty-one**
   three hundred thirteen   **seven hundred ninety-nine**
   six hundred fifty-five   **five hundred sixty**

4. **six hundred eighty**   **eight hundred twenty-one**
   nine hundred nine   **two hundred and fifty-three**
   three hundred twelve

Exercise 7

1. (a) **335**   (b) **420**   (c) **506**

2. (a) **573**   (b) **774**   (c) **508**   (d) **840**

Exercise 8

1. (a) **10**; **10**; **8**; **2** (b)   **11**; **11**; **7**; **4**
   (c) **13**; **13**; **7**; **6** (d)   **14**; **14**; **6**; **8**
   (e) **17**; **17**; **14**; **3**   (f)   **19**; **19**; **9**; **10**
   (g) **25**; **25**; **20**; **5**   (h) **19**; **19**; **13**; **6**

Exercise 9

1. (a) **5; 5**   (b) **7; 7**   (c) **6; 6**

2. (a) **8; 8**   (b) **7; 7**   (c) **9; 9**   (d) **8; 8**
    (e) **4; 4**   (f) **8; 8**

Exercise 10

1. 45 - 31 = **14**

number of buns she made 45	
number sold 31	number left ?

2. 37 - 24 = **13**

    This is a comparison.

red apples 37	
green apples 24	?

3. 23 + 24 = **47**

boy's age 34	younger than father 24
father's age ?	

4. (a) Cost of book + cost of pen = \$32 + \$2 = \$**34**

    (b) Cost of train set - cost of doll = \$23 - \$11 = \$**12**

    (c) Total money - cost of watch = \$86 - \$15 = \$**71**

    (d) Cost of book - total money = \$32 - \$30 = \$**2**

Exercise 11

1. (a) 8; 8   (b) 8; 80   (c) 8; 800

2. (a) 7; 70; 700   (b) 10; 100; 1,000

3.

A5	6		B4	C9		D5	7
8		E5		8	G9		
	H7	5			9		I3
			J6	8		K4	8
L6		M7	7		N7	6	
O9	5			P6	4		

Exercise 12

1.

A 598	C 396	E 787
H 189	M 856	N 495
O 655	R 789	T 971

MEET ME AT THE CORNER

2.

849	667	835
789	798	366
488	569	987

Sentosa Island. The path is the shaded spaces.

3.   410 + 56 = **466**

US› U.S. or 3d› Singapore stamps 410		other stamps 56
total stamps ?		

4.   125 + 63 = **188**

Lily's stickers 125	more 63
brother's stickers ?	

5.   242 + 304 = **546**

books sold 242	books left 304
original number of books ?	

Exercise 13

1.   (a) 6; 6   (b) 6; 60   (c) 6; 600

2.   (a) 4; 40; 400   (b) 9; 90; 900

3.

A 7	B 5		C 2	D 4
E 7		F 3	G 2	3
H 2	I 7		J 1	K 4
	J 6	8	L 8	M 8
N 5		O 5	0	4
P 3	6			Q 2

Exercise 14

1.

657	713	908
120	326	549
834	245	400

2.

A. 305	B. 172
D. 532	C. 256
E. 407	F. 621
H. 410	G. 50
I. 261	J. 813

You will get a picture of a **fish**.

3. 68 - 43 = **25**

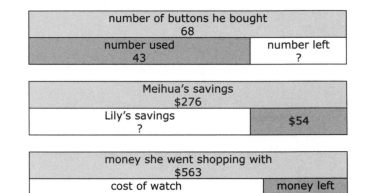

4. $276 - $54 = $**222**

5. $563 - $142 = $**421**

Exercise 15

1. (a) **13**; **33**; **533**   (b) **10**; **50**; **250**
    (c) **13**; **130**; **530**   (d) **10**; **100**; **400**
    (e) **17**; **77**; **277**   (f) **10**; **90**; **390**

2. (a) **71**   (b) **81**   (c) **145**   (d) **640**
    (e) **150**   (f) **100**   (g) **310**   (h) **500**

3. A **81**   B **92**   D **93**
    H **72**   I **82**   P **95**
    R **84**   T **70**   Y **80**

    HAPPY BIRTHDAY

Exercise 16

1. **981   373   471**
    793   872   376
    750   675   890

2. **865   435   826**
    327   787   519
    900   627   318
    Airplane

Exercise 17

1. **91   56   355**
    131   523   480
    824   403   852
    Rabbit

2. 231 + 19 = **250**

original number of cards 231	number given 19
total ?	

3. 285 + 72 = **357**

men 285	women 72
total ?	

4. $162 + $360 = $**522**

Lily's savings $162	Weilin's savings $360
total savings ?	

Exercise 18

1. C **820**   D **325**   E **901**   G **501**
    H **373**   L **640**   T **902**   Z **860**

2. **301   540   764**
    642   700   816
    830   723   915
    615   702   927

3. $82 + $139 = $**221**

money spent $82	money left $139
total money ?	

4. $393 + $438 = $**831**

cost of oven $393	cost of refrigerator $438
total money spent ?	

5. 468 + 156 = **624**

chairs with desks 468	extra chairs 156
total chairs ?	

Exercise 19

1. **327   735**
    691   731   308
    815   725
    GOOD MORNING

2.   95 + 98 + 57 = **250**

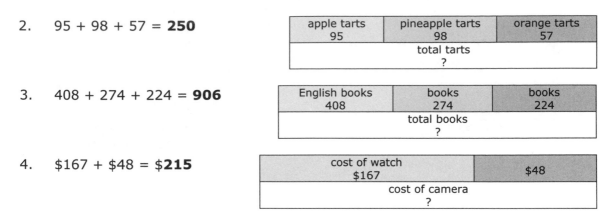

apple tarts 95	pineapple tarts 98	orange tarts 57
total tarts ?		

3.   408 + 274 + 224 = **906**

English books 408	books 274	books 224
total books ?		

4. $167 + $48 = **$215**

cost of watch $167	$48
cost of camera ?	

Exercise 20

1.   C **15**   D **38**   E **37**
      I **39**   M **4**   N **6**
      O **46**   S **28**   T **26**
      IT DOES NOT COME TO ME

2.   A **735**   B **343**   E **26**
      L **363**   M **333**
      N **116**   R **745**   U **540**
      AN UMBRELLA

3. $186 - $38 = **$148**

total money $186	
Money spent $38	money left ?

4.   132 - 34 = **98**

fruit in the basket 132	
rotten 34	not rotten ?

5.   150 - 43 = **107**

Sara's, Sulin's stamps 150	
US› Nicole's, 3d› Meihua's stamps ?	43

Exercise 21

1.   A **454**   B **154**   C **295**
      D **81**   E **522**
      F **352**   G **685**   H **774**
      the treasure is hidden below the rain tree

2.   968 - 395 = **573**

total students 968	
students with glasses 395	students without glasses ?

3. $474 - $282 = $**192**

Meiling's money $474	
sister's money ?	$282

4.   345 - 128 = **217**

This is a comparison.

chicken satay 345	
beef satay 128	?

Exercise 22

US›1. B **253**   S **568**   D **759**
        E **75**   A **217**   O **649**
        0 **579**   K **489**   R **277**
        READ BOOKS

3d›1. A **253**   E **568**   G **759**
        I **75**   N **217**   O **649**
        P **579**   R **489**   S **277**
        MY SINGAPORE

2.   **41   198   269**
      194   195
      512   298   77
      78   374

3.   415 - 158 = **257**

total cookies 415	
given to neighbors 158	left ?

4.   250 - 174 = **76**

US› houses, 3d› flats in Orchid Estate 250	
US› houses, 3d› flats in Rose Estate 174	?

5. $620 - $565 = $**55**

total money $620	
money spent $565	money left ?

Exercise 23

1.

268 I	138 N		
362 T	546 H	26 E	
659 W	26 E	485 L	485 L

2.   700 - 369 = **331**

total 700	
US> cookies, **3d**> fish balls 369	US> muffins, **3d**> prawn balls ?

3.   504 - 286 = **218**

pears 504	
pears sold ?	pears left 286

4.   207 - 179 = **28**

cars in A 207	
cars in B 179	?

Exercise 24

1.   A **81**   C **775**   H **1000**
      I **327**   M **378**   R **530**
      S **277**   S **723**   T **638**

      MERRY **CHRISTMAS**

2.   296 - 158 = **138**

      comparison

cups of coffee 296	
Cups of tea 158	difference ?

3.   150 - 78 = **72**

total balls needed 150	
already made 78	still needed ?

4.   930 - 845 = **85**

stamps collected 930	
stamps left 845	given to friends ?

Review 1

1.   **123   215   649   307   506   780   808   451**

2.   (a) **89**   (b) **367**   (c) **534**   (d) **140**

3. (a) **four hundred and fifty-five**
    (b) **seven hundred and forty-four**
    (c) **eight hundred and fifty**
    (d) **nine hundred and three**

4. (a) **>**   (b) **<**   (c) **>**   (d) **>**   (e) **>**   (f) **>**

5. (a) starting from 100: **58; 88; 99; 59**
    (b) starting from 1000: **360; 500; 20; 450**

6. (a) number of men + number of women = total adults
    287 + 195 = **482**

    (b) number of men - number of women = difference
    287 - 195 = **92**

    (c) adults + children = total people
    482 + 170 = **652**

Exercise 26

1. Answers will vary. Substitute other objects if necessary.

2. (a) **3**   (b) **10**

3. (a) **8**   (b) **11**   (c) **9**   (d) **12**

4. (a) **11**   (b) **9**   (c) **2**   (d) **4**
    (e) **brush**   (f) **clothespin** (**3d**> clothes peg)

5. (a) **m**   (b) **m**   (c) **cm**   (d) **cm**   (e) **m**
    (f) **cm**   (g) **cm**   (h) **cm**   (i) **m**   (j) **cm**

Exercise 27

1. Answers will vary.

2. (a) **12**   (b) **9**   (c) **3**

3. **12; 4**

4. (a) **8**   (b) **11**   (c) **10**   (d) **B**   (e) **A**

3d> Exercise 28

1. Check the lengths of the lines your student draws.

2. AB is 7 cm long.
    (a) The line should be 10 cm long.   (b) The line should be 5 cm long.

US› Exercise 28

1.   (a) **ft**   (b) **in.**   (c) **yd**   (d) **in.**   (e) **ft**

2.   **Yellow rod**

Review 2

1.   (a) 9 tens 9 ones = **99**
     (b) **8** tens **2** ones = 82
     (c) **6** hundreds **4** tens **7** ones = 647
     (d) **5** hundreds **0** tens **3** ones = 503

2.   **899, 904, 908, 910**

3.   Numbers decrease by 10 going down the columns, and increase by 1 going across the row.

994	995	996	997	998	999
	985				
	975		977	**978**	979
	965			968	
	955	956	**957**	**958**	
	945			948	

4.   (a) **>**   (b) **<**   (c) **>**   (d) **>**   (e) **<**   (f) **>**

5.   (a) **157**   (b) **873**   (c) **209**   (d) **920**

6.   **223**

7.   (a) **30**   (b) **42**   (c) **8**   (d) **100**

8.   (a) **1,000** (b) **800**   (c) **690**   (d) **308**   (e) **242**

9.   (a) **349**   (b) **758**   (c) **604**   (d) **580**

10. (a) **two hundred twenty**
     (b) **four hundred thirty-one**
     (c) **eight hundred sixty-nine**
     (d) **nine hundred forty-four**

11. (a) $45 - $26 = **$19**
     (b) $380 + $18 = **$398**
     (c) $26 + $6 + $8 = **$40**

Exercise 29

3.   The **2nd** fruit weighs more than 1 kg.
     The **3rd** fruit weighs 1 kg.
     The **1st** fruit weighs less than 1 kg.

4.   (a) **2**   (b) **3**   (c) **7**   (d) **4**   (e) **1**   (f) **5**

Exercise 30

2. (a) **130**   (b) **90**   (c) **220**   (d) **40**

3. (a) **700**   (b) **200**   (c) **500**   (d) **350**   (e) **200**   (f) **50**

Review 3

1. (a) **192**   (b) **209**   (c) **370**   (d) **405**
    (e) **66**   (f) **605**   (g) **398**   (h) **909**

2. (a) **90**   (b) **7**   (c) **700**   (d) **200**

3. 62 + 38 = 100   100 - 38 = 62
    38 + 62 = 100   100 - 62 = 38

4. (a) **389**   (b) **500**
    (c) **416**   (d) **402**
    (e) **1000**   (f) **55**

5. (a) **528**   (b) **369**   (c) **951**   (d) **369**   (e) **634**

6. Total pages = pages read + pages left to read
                 = 285 + 167 = **452**

7. David's postcards = John's postcards + fewer postcards John had than David
                      = 635 + 165 = **800**

8. Difference = number of apple tarts - number of pineapple tarts
               = 600 – 485 = **115**

9. Total people = sum of number of men, women, and children
                 = 148 + 137 + 359 = **644**

10. Cost of camera = total cost - cost of calculator
                   = $305 - $59 = **$246**

11. Number of beads = number used for handbag + number left
                    = 580 + 8 = **665**

Review 4

1. mango or pear shape

2.

greatest number	smallest number
420	204
431	134
754	457
432	234
954	459
330	303

3. (a) **689**   (b) **40**   (c) **80**   (d) **200**

4.   **12**
     10

5.   (a) **130**
     (b) 210 – 130 = **80**

6.   Number more boys = number of boys - number of girls
                         = 312 - 295 = **17**

7.   Total number = sum of men, women, and children
                    = 292 + 149 + 68 = **509**

8.   Amount sister saved = total amount - amount Meihua saved
                           = $502 - $348 = **$154**

9.   Money needed = cost of machine - money now
                     = $650 - $527 = **$123**

10. Weight of mango = weight of papaya - difference in weight
                       = 860 g - 280 g **= 580 g**

11. Total length = sum of length of the 3 sides
                     = 34 cm + 28 cm + 16 cm = **78 cm**

Exercise 31

1.   (a) **24; 24**   (b) **24; 24**   (c) **20; 20**
2.   (a) **14; 14**   (b) **14; 14**   (c) **20; 20**
3.   (a) 7 x 3 = **21**   (b) 9 x 4 = **36**

Exercise 32

1.   **10**   2.   **8**   3.   **18**
4.   **24**   5.   **28**

Exercise 33

1.   **20**   2.   **12**   3.   **24**
4.   **24**   5.   **18**   6.   **50**

Exercise 34

1.   (a) **15; 15**   (b) **14; 14**   (c) **18; 18**
2.   (a) **30; 30**   (b) **28; 28**   (c) **48; 48**   (d) **30; 30**

Exercise 35

1. (a) **6**   (b) **8**   (c) **4**
2. (a) **5**   (b) **5**
3. (a) **6**   (b) **6**
4. **4**

Exercise 36

1. (a) **6**   (b) **7**   (c) **3**
2. **32 ÷ 4 = 8; 8**
3. **30 ÷ 6 = 5; 5**

Exercise 37

1. (a) **3**   (b) **4**   (c) **6**
2. (a) **3**   (b) **3**
3. (a) **7**   (b) **7**
4. **3**

Exercise 38

1. (a) **2**   (b) **4**   (c) **3**
2. **18 ÷ 2 = 9; 9**
3. **15 ÷ 3 = 5; 5**

Exercise 39

1. (a) **6; 6**   (b) **5; 5**

2. (a) **3; 2**   (b) **7; 3**   (c) **5; 4**   (d) **9; 2**

3. (a) **35 ÷ 7 = 5; 35 ÷ 5 = 7**
   (b) **18 ÷ 6 = 3; 18 ÷ 3 = 6**

4. **6 x 4 = 24**   **4 x 6 = 24;**
   24 ÷ 6 = 4   **24 ÷ 4 = 6**

Review 5

1.   **24 + 17 = 41**   **17 + 24 = 41**
     41 - 17 = 24   **41 - 24 = 17**

2.   **8 x 2 = 16**   **2 x 8 = 16**
     16 ÷ 2 = 8   **16 ÷ 8 = 2**

3.   (a) The numbers decrease by 10.

750	740	**730**	720	**710**	700	**690**

     (b) The numbers increase by 100.

392	**492**	592	**692**	792	**892**	992

4.   (a) **465**   (b) **261**   (c) **397**   (d) **742**
     (e) **44**   (f) **665**   (g) **738**   (h) **199**

5.   (a) **957**   (b) **980**   (c) **980**   (d) **957**

6.   **20 ÷ 5 = 4; 4**

7.   **18 ÷ 6 = 3; 3**

8.   **5 x 4 = 20; 20**

9.   Number of blue balloons = total balloons - red balloons
                 = 124 - 48 **= 76**

10.   Sufen's height = Meihua's height + difference in height
               = 98 cm + 14 cm **= 112** cm

11.   Weight of other apple = total weight - weight of one apple
               = 290 g - 132 g **= 158** g

Exercise 40

1.   **2; 4; 6; 8; 10; 12; 14; 16; 18; 20**

2.   **8; 10; 12; 14; 16; 18; 20**

3.   **4; 6; 8; 10; 12; 14; 16; 18; 20**

Exercise 41

1.   **6; 6**

2.   **8; 8**

3.   **10; 10**

4.   **12; 12**

5.   **2 x 7 = 14; 14**

6.   **2 x 8 = 16; 16**

Exercise 42

1. (a) **8**   (b) **12**   (c) **14; 16**

2. **6; 8; 10; 12; 14; 16; 18; 20**

Exercise 43

1. 2 x 2 = **4**
    2 x 3 = **6**
    2 x 1 = **2**
    2 x 6 = **12**
    2 x 4 = **8**
    2 x 9 = **18**
    2 x 5 = **10**
    2 x 7 = **14**
    2 x 10 = **20**
    2 x 8 – **16**

Exercise 44

1. (a) **12; 12**   (b) **14; 14**   (c) **18; 18**   (d) **20; 20**

2. 10 x 2 = 20 = 2 x 10
    5 x 2 = 10 = 2 x 5
    7 x 2 = 14 = 2 x 7
    3 x 2 = 6 = 2 x 3
    9 x 2 = 18 = 2 x 9
    6 x 2 = 12 = 2 x 6
    8 x 2 = 16 = 2 x 8

Exercise 45

1. down: 8; 16; 6; 18
             20; 4; 12
             10; 14; 2
2. down: 6; 8; 20; 16
             16; 18; 10; 18
             12; 14; 8; 12

Exercise 46
(Only one equation is shown here using the number of equal parts first. Students may also have the related equation for each. For example, #2 could be calculated as the cost of each car x the number of toy cars to give the equation 2 x 6 = 12.)

1.   Total buns = number of boxes x number of buns in each box = **2 x 8 = 16**

2.   Total paid = number of toy cars x cost of each car = **6 x $2 = $12**

3.   Total number of shirts = number of children x number of shirts for each
                        = **3 x 2 = 6**

4.   Total cost = number of tins x cost of each tin = 2 x $7 = **$14**

5.   Total kilograms = number of tins x weight of each tin = 5 x 2 kg = **10** kg

6.   Total length = number of sides x length of each side = 2 x 4 m = **8** m

---

Exercise 47

1.   **3; 6; 9; 12; 15; 18; 21; 24; 27; 30**

2.   **12; 15; 18; 21; 24; 27; 30**

Exercise 48

1.   **6; 9; 12; 15; 18; 21; 24; 27; 30**

2.   (a) **4; 8; 12; 16**   (b) **6; 15; 21; 27**
      (c) **$6; $10; $14; $18; $20**   (d) **$9; $12; $18; $24; $30**

Exercise 49

1.   **6; 6**

2.   (a) **9**   (b) **12; 12**   (c) **15; 15**

3.   (a) **18; 18**   (b) **21; 21**   (c) **24; 24**   (d) **27; 27**

Exercise 50

1. $1 \times 3 = \mathbf{3} = 3 \times 1$
        $4 \times 3 = \mathbf{12} = 3 \times 4$
        $8 \times 3 = \mathbf{24} = 3 \times 8$
        $2 \times 3 = \mathbf{6} = 3 \times 2$
        $9 \times 3 = \mathbf{27} = 3 \times 9$
        $7 \times 3 = \mathbf{21} = 3 \times 7$
        $6 \times 3 = \mathbf{18} = 3 \times 6$

2.   3 = 1 x 3   18 = 3 x 6
         6 = 2 x 3   21 = 7 x 3
         9 = 3 x 3   24 = 3 x 8
       12 = 4 x 3   27 = 3 x 9
       15 = 5 x 3   30 = 10 x 3

Exercise 51

1.   (a) **12**   (b) **18**   (c) **24; 27**

2.   **9; 12; 15; 18; 21; 24; 27; 30**

Exercise 52

1.   (a) **12**   (b) **18**   (c) **30; 27**

2.   **24; 21; 18; 15; 12; 9; 6; 3**

Exercise 53

1.   **12**   **24**   **18**
     9   **21**   **27**
    15   **12**   **27**
    30   **24**   **18**

Exercise 54

1.   3 x 10 = 30   **30** eggs

2.   3 x 8 = 24   **24** m

3.   3 x 5 = 15 $**15**

4.   3 x 7 = 21   **21** days

5.   3 x 9 = 27   **27** (**US›** **in., 3d›** cm)

6.   6 x 3 = 18   **18** kg

Exercise 55

1.   6   12
     18   24
     30   10
      8   15
     14   21
     27   12

2.   8 x 3 = 24   **24** rooms

3.   7 x 3 = 21   **21** oranges

4.   7 x 2 = 14   **14** copies

5.   2 x 10 = 20   **20** kg

6.   8 x 2 = 16   **16** m

7.   3 x 6 = 18 $**18**

Exercise 56

1.   **1**   **2**
     5   **8; 8**
     3; 3   **9; 9**
     10; 10   **4; 4**
     6; 6   **7; 7**

2.   **1; 5; 2; 4; 8; 6; 10; 7; 9**

Exercise 57

1.   Total = 8 children. Number of parts = 2 groups. Children in each part = ?
     8 ÷ 2 = 4   ? = **4** children

2.   Whole = 10 buns.   Number of parts = 2 boxes.   Buns in each part = ?
     10 ÷ 2 = 5   ? = **5** buns

3.   Whole = 12 pencils.   Number of parts = 2 boys.   Pencils in each part = ?
     12 ÷ 2 = 6   ? = **6** pencils

4.   Whole = 20 chairs.   Number of parts = 2 rows.   Chairs in each row = ?
     20 ÷ 2 = 10   ? = **10** chairs

5.   Whole = 14 m.   Length in each part = 2 m.   Number of pieces of rope = ?
     14 ÷ 2 = 7   ? = **7** pieces

6.   Whole = 16 pies. Number of pies in each part = 2. Number of boxes = ?
     16 ÷ 2 = 8   ? = **8** boxes

Exercise 58

1.   **1**
                   2
     4   **4**
     5   **5**
     3   **3**
     10   **10**
     7   **7**
     9   **9**
     6   **6**
     8   **8**

2. 6 ÷ 3 → 2   10 → 30 ÷ 3
    18 ÷ 3 → 6   5 → 15 ÷ 3
    24 ÷ 3 → 8   3 → 9 ÷ 3
    12 ÷ 3 → 4   1 → 3 ÷ 3
    27 ÷ 3 → 9   7 → 21 ÷ 3

Exercise 59

1. Whole = 24.   Number of parts = 3 rows.   Children in each part = ?
    24 ÷ 3 = 8   ? = **8** children

2. Total = $18.   Number of parts = 3 weeks.   Money in each week = ?
    18 ÷ 3 = 6   ? = **$6**

3. Whole = 12 **US›** yd, **3d›** m.   Number of pieces = 3.   Length of each piece = ?
    12 ÷ 3 = 4   ? = **US› 4 yd, 3d› 4 m**

4. Whole = 15 m.   Length in each part = 3 m.   Number of dresses = ?
    15 ÷ 3 = 5   ? = **5** dresses

5. Whole = 27 pears.   Number of parts = 3.   Pears in each part = ?
    27 ÷ 3 = 9   ? = **9** pears

6. Whole = $21.   Number of parts (kg) = 3.   Cost for each part = ?
    21 ÷ 3 = 7   ? = $**7**

Exercise 60

1. 3 › 9 ÷ 3   12 ÷ 2 ← 6
    2 → 6 ÷ 3   15 ÷ 3 ← 5
    1 → 2 ÷ 2   20 ÷ 2 ←- 10
    4 → 12 ÷ 3   16 ÷ 2 ← 8
    7 → 14 ÷ 2   27 ÷ 3 ← 9

2.

6 ÷ 3	14 ÷ 2
2	**7**
D	**O**

12 ÷ 2	21 ÷ 3	27 ÷ 3
6	**7**	**9**
N	**O**	**T**

20 ÷ 2	3 ÷ 3	24 ÷ 3	18 ÷ 2	9 ÷ 3
10	**1**	**8**	**9**	**3**
W	**A**	**S**	**T**	**E**

27 ÷ 3	12 ÷ 3	15 ÷ 3	6 ÷ 2
9	**4**	**5**	**3**
T	**I**	**M**	**E**

Exercise 61

1. Whole = $24. Number of parts (1 kg) = 3 parts. Money for each part = ?
    24 ÷ 3 = 8   ? = **$8**

2. Whole = 18 cakes. Number of parts = 2 boxes. Number of cakes in each box = ?
    18 ÷ 2 = 9   ? = **9** cakes

3. Whole = 18 notebooks.   Number in each part (which costs $1) = 3.
    Number $1 parts = ?
    18 ÷ 3 = 6   ? = **$6**

4. Whole = $12.   Amount in each part (1 kg) = $2.   Number of 1 kg part= ?
    12 ÷ 2 = 6   ? = **6 kg**

5. Whole = $27. Number of parts = 3 weeks. Money spent in each week: ?
    27 ÷ 3 = 9   ? = **$9**

6. Whole = $16.   Number of parts = 2 people.   Amount in each part = ?
    16 ÷ 2 = 8   ? = **$8**

Exercise 62

1. **10**   **18**   **4**   **8**

    12   **7**   **10**   **14**

    16   **7**   **9**   **27**

2. Whole = length of string, 15 cm.   Number of parts = 3 pieces
    We need to find the number of cm in each piece. We divide.
    15 ÷ 3 = 5   The length of each piece of string is **5** cm.

3. Number of parts = 7 bundles.   Number of bars of soap in each part = 3
    We need to find the total number of bars of soap. We multiply.
    3 x 7 = 21   There are **21** bars of soap altogether.

4. Number of parts = 3 boys.   Number of cars for each part (boy) = 4
    We need to find the total number of cars. We multiply.
    3 x 4 = 12   They bought **12** toy cars altogether.

5. Number of parts = 6 dresses.   Length for each part = 3 (**US›** yd, **3d›** m)
    We need to find the total length of cloth. We multiply.
    6 x 3 = 18   She needs **18 (US› yd, 3d› m)** of cloth.

6. Total cost = $24.   Number of parts = 3 tickets.
    We need to find the cost of each part. We divide.
    24 ÷ 3 = 8   The cost of each ticket is **$8**.

7. Total money = $18.   Number of parts (boys) = 2
    We need to find the amount of money for each boy. We divide.
    18 ÷ 2 = 9   Each boy spent **$9**.

Review 6

1. (a) **eight hundred fifty-seven**
   (b) **six hundred forty-four**

2. **6 x 3 = 18**   **18 ÷ 6 = 3**
   3 x 6 = 18   **18 ÷ 3 = 6**

3. (a) **456 - 50 = 406** or **456 - 406 = 50**
   (b) **275 + 325 = 600** or **325 + 275 = 600**
   (c) **3 x 9 = 27** or **9 x 3 = 27**
   (d) **18 ÷ 9 = 2** or **18 ÷ 2 = 9**

4. Increases by tens across, decreases by ones down.

950	960	970	**980**	990	**1000**
	959			989	
	958			**988**	
	957			987	
946	**956**	966	976	**986**	**996**

5. (a) **7; 7**   (b) **6; 6**

6. **829; 831; 846; 852**

7. (a) **7**   (b) **50**

8. **440**   **96**   **230**
   103   **450**   **636**
   330   **352**   **840**
   320   **455**   **518**
   lion's head

9. **10; 12; 6; 4; 8; 16; 14; 7; 9; 18; 20; 10; 8; 6; 12; 10; 20**

10. 402 - 35 = 367   **367** mangoes

11. 6 x $4 - $24 $**24**

12. 24 ÷ 3 = 8   **8** soldiers

13. 460 - 295 = 165   **165** more chickens

14. 18 ÷ 2 = 9   **9** (**US**> pastries, **3d**> curry puffs)

15. 285 + 168 = 453   **453** sticks

Review 7

1. (a) **550**   (b) **929**

2. (a) **seven hundred forty-four**
   (b) **eight hundred six**

3. (a) <   (b) <
    (c) >   (d) >
    (e) >   (f) <

4. (a) **879**   (b) **760**   (c) **504**
    (d) **90**   (e) **607**   (f) **10**

5. (a) **3**   (b) 3 x 4 = **12**

6. (a) **4**   (b) 3 x 4 = **12**

US> 7.   (a) **lb**   (b) **in.**   (c) **oz**   (d) **yd**   (e) **ft**
3d> 7.   (a) **kg**   (b) **cm**   (c) **g**   (d) **m**

8. (a) **473**   (b) **516**
    (c) **852**   (d) **800**
    (e) **340**   (f) **126**
    (g) **358**   (h) **575**

9. (a) **6**   (b) **15**
    (c) **21**   (d) **18**
    (e) **9**   (f) **10**
    (g) **16**   (h) **27**
    (i) **1**   (j) **2**
    (k) **5**   (l) **9**
    (m) **1**   (n) **5**
    (o) **8**   (p) **7**

10. 12 ÷ 2 = 6   **6** (**US>** lb, **3d>** kg)

11. 6 x 3 = 18 $**18**

12. 18 - 3 = 15   **15** (**US>** yd, **3d>** m)

13. 500 - 264 = 236 $**236**

14. 85 + 46 = 131   **131** marbles

15. 420 - 285 = 135   **135** women

Answers to Mental Math

Mental Math 1

+	1	2	3	4	5	6	7	8	9
1	2	3	4	5	6	7	8	9	10
2	3	4	5	6	7	8	9	10	11
3	4	5	6	7	8	9	10	11	12
4	5	6	7	8	9	10	11	12	13
5	6	7	8	9	10	11	12	13	14
6	7	8	9	10	11	12	13	14	15
7	8	9	10	11	12	13	14	15	16
8	9	10	11	12	13	14	15	16	17
9	10	11	12	13	14	15	16	17	18

Mental Math 2

+	2	9	7	4	1	5	3	8	6
3	5	12	10	7	4	8	6	11	9
7	9	16	14	11	8	12	10	15	13
4	6	13	11	8	5	9	7	12	10
2	4	11	9	6	3	7	5	10	8
6	8	15	13	10	7	11	9	14	12
9	11	18	16	13	10	14	12	17	15
1	3	10	8	5	2	6	4	9	7
5	7	14	12	9	6	10	8	13	11
8	10	17	15	12	9	13	11	16	14

Mental Math 3

+	9	6	3	1	5	2	4	8	7
4	13	10	7	5	9	6	8	12	11
6	15	12	9	7	11	8	10	14	13
5	14	11	8	6	10	7	9	13	12
9	18	15	12	10	14	11	13	17	16
2	11	8	5	3	7	4	6	10	9
3	12	9	6	4	8	5	7	11	10
7	16	13	10	8	12	9	11	15	14
1	10	7	4	2	6	3	5	9	8
8	17	14	11	9	13	10	12	16	15

Mental Math 4

#		#	
1.	2	16.	13
2.	4	17.	13
3.	6	18.	15
4.	8	19.	11
5.	10	20.	14
6.	14	21.	11
7.	16	22.	15
8.	18	23.	11
9.	20	24.	14
10.	11	25.	13
11.	14	26.	12
12.	12	27.	13
13.	12	28.	14
14.	16	29.	13
15.	14	30.	12

Mental Math 5

#		#	
1.	3	16.	16
2.	6	17.	14
3.	9	18.	14
4.	12	19.	15
5.	15	20.	11
6.	18	21.	13
7.	21	22.	18
8.	24	23.	17
9.	27	24.	13
10.	30	25.	15
11.	15	26.	15
12.	12	27.	16
13.	12	28.	13
14.	16	29.	13
15.	14	30.	17

Mental Math 6

#		#	
1.	18	16.	5
2.	16	17.	5
3.	14	18.	3
4.	12	19.	6
5.	10	20.	6
6.	8	21.	8
7.	6	22.	6
8.	4	23.	7
9.	2	24.	9
10.	0	25.	5
11.	7	26.	3
12.	7	27.	9
13.	2	28.	9
14.	4	29.	4
15.	8	30.	8

Mental Math 7

#		#	
1.	27	16.	5
2.	24	17.	9
3.	21	18.	9
4.	18	19.	6
5.	15	20.	13
6.	12	21.	8
7.	9	22.	9
8.	6	23.	3
9.	3	24.	7
10.	0	25.	6
11.	7	26.	4
12.	8	27.	8
13.	8	28.	9
14.	4	29.	9
15.	6	30.	4

Mental Math 8

#		#	
1.	21	14.	82
2.	67	15.	56
3.	61	16.	30
4.	54	17.	72
5.	63	18.	44
6.	21	19.	54
7.	63	20.	37
8.	95	21.	91
9.	90	22.	40
10.	33	23.	88
11.	52	24.	20
12.	30	25.	72
13.	45	26.	81

2, 4, 6, 8, 10
12, 14. 16, 18, 20

Mental Math 9

#		#	
1.	82	16.	35
2.	26	17.	75
3.	15	18.	24
4.	66	19.	88
5.	78	20.	58
6.	19	21.	65
7.	56	22.	47
8.	58	23.	47
9.	44	24.	14
10.	87	25.	77
11.	39	26.	36
12.	23	27.	29
13.	46	28.	63
14.	67	29.	39
15.	58	30.	20

Mental Math 10

#		#	
1.	31	13.	65
2.	58	14.	65
3.	91	15.	23
4.	42	16.	96
5.	51	17.	82
6.	89	18.	58
7.	44	19.	84
8.	76	20.	70
9.	41	21.	37
10.	69	22.	44
11.	38	23.	47
12.	70	24.	91

3, 6, 9, 12,
15, 18, 21,
24, 27, 30

Mental Math 11

#		#	
1.	90	16.	130
2.	60	17.	130
3.	80	18.	150
4.	80	19.	110
5.	100	20.	140
6.	140	21.	110
7.	570	22.	150
8.	280	23.	110
9.	370	24.	140
10.	110	25.	130
11.	140	26.	120
12.	120	27.	130
13.	120	28.	140
14.	160	29.	130
15.	140	30.	120

Mental Math 12

	Mental Math 12		
1.	432	16.	623
2.	234	17.	533
3.	766	18.	865
4.	978	19.	150
5.	190	20.	497
6.	311	21.	311
7.	413	22.	225
8.	770	23.	629
9.	920	24.	544
10.	191	25.	883
11.	494	26.	210
12.	532	27.	323
13.	882	28.	555
14.	736	29.	953
15.	274	30.	112

	Mental Math 13		
1.	60	16.	60
2.	160	17.	50
3.	90	18.	30
4.	50	19.	140
5.	150	20.	60
6.	70	21.	80
7.	80	22.	60
8.	180	23.	70
9.	30	24.	90
10.	330	25.	50
11.	50	26.	30
12.	70	27.	90
13.	20	28.	90
14.	40	29.	40
15.	80	30.	80

	Mental Math 14		
1.	70	14.	90
2.	10	15.	60
3.	50	16.	120
4.	30	17.	80
5.	90	18.	90
6.	50	19.	30
7.	120	20.	140
8.	50	21.	60
9.	110	22.	40
10.	80	23.	80
11.	80	24.	130
12.	100	25.	140
13.	60	26.	40

20, 18, 16, 14, 12,
10, 8, 6, 4, 2

	Mental Math 15		
1.	70	13.	150
2.	240	14.	50
3.	110	15.	80
4.	20	16.	160
5.	150	17.	120
6.	140	18.	90
7.	140	19.	130
8.	120	20.	100
9.	110	21.	170
10.	60	22.	140
11.	80	23.	80
12.	100	24.	110

30, 27, 24,
21, 18, 15, 12,
9, 6, 3

	Mental Math 16		
1.	927	16.	705
2.	624	17.	894
3.	422	18.	509
4.	118	19.	376
5.	815	20.	214
6.	716	21.	968
7.	598	22.	619
8.	445	23.	553
9.	237	24.	297
10.	189	25.	926
11.	197	26.	704
12.	408	27.	868
13.	648	28.	959
14.	335	29.	503
15.	706	30.	424

	Mental Math 17		
1.	131	16.	365
2.	558	17.	265
3.	691	18.	423
4.	842	19.	796
5.	251	20.	182
6.	489	21.	958
7.	343	22.	584
8.	776	23.	670
9.	641	24.	937
10.	169	25.	844
11.	238	26.	347
12.	570	27.	491
13.	644	28.	884
14.	731	29.	865
15.	992	30.	196

	Mental Math 18
1.	10
2.	15
3.	9
4.	9
5.	6
6.	0
7.	12
8.	6
9.	7
10.	12
11.	12
12.	18
13.	13
14.	0

10, 12, 14, 16, 18

	Mental Math 19
1.	100
2.	150
3.	90
4.	80
5.	70
6.	30
7.	130
8.	60
9.	60
10.	130
11.	140
12.	210
13.	10
14.	280

16, 18, 20, 22, 24

	Mental Math 20
1.	36
2.	37
3.	51
4.	47
5.	8
6.	56
7.	31
8.	81
9.	111
10.	115
11.	70
12.	45
13.	8
14.	35

12, 15, 18, 21, 24

Mental Math 21

1.	937	15.	186
2.	693	16.	381
3.	215	17.	130
4.	492	18.	278
5.	779	19.	574
6.	421	20.	361
7.	513	21.	185
8.	444	22.	432
9.	667	23.	966
10.	248	24.	719
11.	861	25.	375
12.	914	26.	443
13.	586	27.	692
14.	727	28.	828
12, 15, 18, 21, 24, 27, 30			

Mental Math 22

1.	761	12.	454
2.	344	13.	418
3.	492	14.	58
4.	878	15.	101
5.	338	16.	20
6.	383	17.	1000
7.	659	18.	305
8.	812	19.	320
9.	871	20.	374
10.	59	21.	984
11.	72	22.	705
23.	411		
24.	695		
25.	900		
26	467		

Mental Math 23

x	1	2	3	4	5	6	7	8	9	10
1	1	2	3	4	5	6	7	8	9	10
2	2	4	6	8	10	12	14	16	18	20
3	3	6								
4	4	8								
5	5	10								
6	6	12								
7	7	14								
8	8	16								
9	9	18								
10	10	20								

Mental Math 24

x	5	10	2	1	8	9	3	7	4	6
1	5	10	2	1	8	9	3	7	4	6
2	10	20	4	2	16	18	6	14	8	12

x	3	6	1	9	5	4	7	10	8	2
2	6	12	2	18	10	8	14	20	16	4
1	3	6	1	9	5	4	7	10	8	2

x	1	4	5	2	7	3	8	9	6	1
1	1	4	5	2	7	3	8	9	6	1
2	2	8	10	4	14	6	16	18	12	2

Mental Math 25			
1.	1	16.	8
2.	12	17.	2
3.	16	18.	14
4.	5	19.	3
5.	9	20.	20
6.	4	21.	6
7.	8	22.	4
8.	18	23.	4
9.	6	24.	10
10.	10	25.	7
11.	4	26.	18
12.	6	27.	6
13.	16	28.	14
14.	5	29.	8
15.	16	30.	12

Mental Math 26

x	1	2	3	4	5	6	7	8	9	10
1	1	2	3	4	5	6	7	8	9	10
2	2	4	6	8	10	12	14	16	18	20
3	3	6	9	12	15	18	21	24	27	30
4	4	8	12							
5	5	10	15							
6	6	12	18							
7	7	14	21							
8	8	16	24							
9	9	18	27							
10	10	20	30							

Mental Math 27

x	5	10	2	1	8	9	3	7	4	6
1	5	10	2	1	8	9	3	7	4	6
2	10	20	4	2	16	18	6	14	8	12
3	15	30	6	3	24	27	9	21	12	18

x	3	6	1	9	5	4	7	10	8	2
2	6	12	2	18	10	8	14	20	16	4
1	3	6	1	9	5	4	7	10	8	2
3	9	18	3	27	15	12	21	30	24	6

x	1	4	5	2	7	3	8	9	6	1
1	1	4	5	2	7	3	8	9	6	1
3	3	12	15	6	21	9	24	27	18	3
2	2	8	10	4	14	6	16	18	12	2

Mental Math 28

1.	3	16.	6
2.	10	17.	6
3.	12	18.	27
4.	20	19.	12
5.	15	20.	27
6.	8	21.	9
7.	24	22.	4
8.	30	23.	18
9.	16	24.	14
10.	21	25.	18
11.	14	26.	16
12.	15	27.	24
13.	30	28.	18
14.	21	29.	18
15.	27	30.	12

Mental Math 29

1.	8	16.	10
2.	1	17.	10
3.	4	18.	7
4.	9	19.	5
5.	2	20.	6
6.	3	21.	3
7.	7	22.	9
8.	2	23.	5
9.	4	24.	8
10.	6	25.	1
11.	3	26.	5
12.	7	27.	8
13.	6	28.	4
14.	2	29.	9
15.	36	30.	458

Mental Math 30

1.	9	16.	3
2.	1	17.	3
3.	5	18.	10
4.	4	19.	1
5.	10	20.	8
6.	2	21.	2
7.	7	22.	4
8.	8	23.	5
9.	7	24.	6
10.	7	25.	6
11.	2	26.	7
12.	8	27.	3
13.	5	28.	1
14.	9	29.	6
15.	10	30.	4

Mental Math 31

1.	8	16.	6
2.	10	17.	20
3.	8	18.	3
4.	30	19.	1
5.	7	20.	15
6.	9	21.	9
7.	18	22.	21
8.	18	23.	2
9.	6	24.	6
10.	24	25.	10
11.	21	26.	4
12.	5	27.	6
13.	14	28.	3
14.	9	29.	9
15.	12	30.	12

Mental Math 32

1.	16	16.	9
2.	27	17.	8
3.	7	18.	3
4.	4	19.	8
5.	24	20.	16
6.	21	21.	9
7.	7	22.	6
8.	18	23.	6
9.	2	24.	6
10.	4	25.	7
11.	18	26.	12
12.	8	27.	27
13.	14	28.	1
14.	10	29.	2
15.	324	30.	84

Mental Math 1

+	1	2	3	4	5	6	7	8	9
1									
2									
3									
4									
5									
6									
7									
8									
9									

Mental Math 2

+	2	9	7	4	1	5	3	8	6
3									
7									
4									
2									
6									
9									
1									
5									
8									

Mental Math 3

+	9	6	3	1	5	2	4	8	7
4									
6									
5									
9									
2									
3									
7									
1									
8									

Mental Math 4

1. $0 + 2 =$ _____

2. $2 + 2 =$ _____

3. $4 + 2 =$ _____

4. $6 + 2 =$ _____

5. $8 + 2 =$ _____

6. $12 + 2 =$ _____

7. $14 + 2 =$ _____

8. $16 + 2 =$ _____

9. $18 + 2 =$ _____

10. $5 + 6 =$ _____

11. $7 + 7 =$ _____

12. $8 + 4 =$ _____

13. $6 + 6 =$ _____

14. $7 + 9 =$ _____

15. $9 + 5 =$ _____

16. $8 + 5 =$ _____

17. $6 + 7 =$ _____

18. $7 + 8 =$ _____

19. $8 + 3 =$ _____

20. $5 + 9 =$ _____

21. $7 + 4 =$ _____

22. $6 + 9 =$ _____

23. $6 + 5 =$ _____

24. $8 + 6 =$ _____

25. $6 + 7 =$ _____

26. $7 + 5 =$ _____

27. $5 + 8 =$ _____

28. $6 + 8 =$ _____

29. $7 + 6 =$ _____

30. $5 + 7 =$ _____

Mental Math 5

1. $0 + 3 =$ _____

2. $3 + 3 =$ _____

3. $6 + 3 =$ _____

4. $9 + 3 =$ _____

5. $12 + 3 =$ _____

6. $15 + 3 =$ _____

7. $18 + 3 =$ _____

8. $21 + 3 =$ _____

9. $24 + 3 =$ _____

10. $27 + 3 =$ _____

11. $8 + 7 =$ _____

12. $9 + 3 =$ _____

13. $7 + 5 =$ _____

14. $9 + 7 =$ _____

15. $6 + 8 =$ _____

16. $7 + 9 =$ _____

17. $9 + 5 =$ _____

18. $5 + 9 =$ _____

19. $9 + 6 =$ _____

20. $9 + 2 =$ _____

21. $5 + 8 =$ _____

22. $9 + 9 =$ _____

23. $8 + 9 =$ _____

24. $7 + 6 =$ _____

25. $7 + 8 =$ _____

26. $6 + 9 =$ _____

27. $8 + 8 =$ _____

28. $5 + 8 =$ _____

29. $9 + 4 =$ _____

30. $9 + 8 =$ _____

Mental Math 6

1. $20 - 2 =$ _____

2. $18 - 2 =$ _____

3. $16 - 2 =$ _____

4. $14 - 2 =$ _____

5. $12 - 2 =$ _____

6. $10 - 2 =$ _____

7. $8 - 2 =$ _____

8. $6 - 2 =$ _____

9. $4 - 2 =$ _____

10. $2 - 2 =$ _____

11. $11 - 4 =$ _____

12. $12 - 5 =$ _____

13. $11 - 9 =$ _____

14. $12 - 8 =$ _____

15. $13 - 5 =$ _____

16. $11 - 6 =$ _____

17. $12 - 7 =$ _____

18. $11 - 8 =$ _____

19. $12 - 6 =$ _____

20. $13 - 7 =$ _____

21. $12 - 4 =$ _____

22. $11 - 5 =$ _____

23. $13 - 6 =$ _____

24. $12 - 3 =$ _____

25. $13 - 8 =$ _____

26. $12 - 9 =$ _____

27. $13 - 4 =$ _____

28. $11 - 2 =$ _____

29. $13 - 9 =$ _____

30. $11 - 3 =$ _____

Mental Math 7

1. $30 - 3 =$ _____

2. $27 - 3 =$ _____

3. $24 - 3 =$ _____

4. $21 - 3 =$ _____

5. $18 - 3 =$ _____

6. $15 - 3 =$ _____

7. $12 - 3 =$ _____

8. $9 - 3 =$ _____

9. $6 - 3 =$ _____

10. $3 - 3 =$ _____

11. $14 - 7 =$ _____

12. $16 - 8 =$ _____

13. $17 - 9 =$ _____

14. $13 - 9 =$ _____

15. $13 - 7 =$ _____

16. $14 - 9 =$ _____

17. $16 - 7 =$ _____

18. $14 - 5 =$ _____

19. $15 - 9 =$ _____

20. $19 - 6 =$ _____

21. $14 - 6 =$ _____

22. $15 - 6 =$ _____

23. $12 - 9 =$ _____

24. $16 - 9 =$ _____

25. $14 - 8 =$ _____

26. $13 - 9 =$ _____

27. $15 - 7 =$ _____

28. $18 - 9 =$ _____

29. $17 - 8 =$ _____

30. $12 - 8 =$ _____

Mental Math 8

1. $14 + 7 =$ _____

2. $62 + 5 =$ _____

3. $55 + 6 =$ _____

4. $49 + 5 =$ _____

5. $56 + 7 =$ _____

6. $15 + 6 =$ _____

7. $54 + 9 =$ _____

8. $87 + 8 =$ _____

9. $81 + 9 =$ _____

10. $25 + 8 =$ _____

11. $47 + 5 =$ _____

12. $25 + 5 =$ _____

13. $36 + 9 =$ _____

14. $76 + 6 =$ _____

15. $49 + 7 =$ _____

16. $27 + 3 =$ _____

17. $69 + 3 =$ _____

18. $38 + 6 =$ _____

19. $47 + 7 =$ _____

20. $28 + 9 =$ _____

21. $83 + 8 =$ _____

22. $38 + 2 =$ _____

23. $79 + 9 =$ _____

24. $16 + 4 =$ _____

25. $68 + 4 =$ _____

26. $72 + 9 =$ _____

Fill in the missing numbers:

1, _____ , 3, _____ , 5, _____ , 7, _____ , 9, _____

11, _____ , 13, _____ , 15, _____ , 17, _____ , 19, _____

Mental Math 9

1. $91 - 9 =$ _____

2. $34 - 8 =$ _____

3. $22 - 7 =$ _____

4. $75 - 9 =$ _____

5. $83 - 5 =$ _____

6. $26 - 7 =$ _____

7. $63 - 7 =$ _____

8. $64 - 6 =$ _____

9. $52 - 8 =$ _____

10. $93 - 6 =$ _____

11. $44 - 5 =$ _____

12. $31 - 8 =$ _____

13. $51 - 5 =$ _____

14. $76 - 9 =$ _____

15. $65 - 7 =$ _____

16. $41 - 6 =$ _____

17. $84 - 9 =$ _____

18. $31 - 7 =$ _____

19. $97 - 9 =$ _____

20. $66 - 8 =$ _____

21. $73 - 8 =$ _____

22. $52 - 5 =$ _____

23. $54 - 7 =$ _____

24. $23 - 9 =$ _____

25. $85 - 8 =$ _____

26. $42 - 6 =$ _____

27. $35 - 6 =$ _____

28. $72 - 9 =$ _____

29. $47 - 8 =$ _____

30. $28 - 8 =$ _____

Mental Math 10

1. $40 - 9 =$ _____

2. $49 + 9 =$ _____

3. $86 + 5 =$ _____

4. $50 - 8 =$ _____

5. $46 + 5 =$ _____

6. $97 - 8 =$ _____

7. $35 + 9 =$ _____

8. $80 - 4 =$ _____

9. $32 + 9 =$ _____

10. $70 - 1 =$ _____

11. $46 - 8 =$ _____

12. $65 + 5 =$ _____

13. $57 + 8 =$ _____

14. $68 - 3 =$ _____

15. $30 - 7 =$ _____

16. $88 + 8 =$ _____

17. $76 + 6 =$ _____

18. $60 - 2 =$ _____

19. $90 - 6 =$ _____

20. $64 + 6 =$ _____

21. $28 + 9 =$ _____

22. $37 + 7 =$ _____

23. $50 - 3 =$ _____

24. $83 + 8 =$ _____

Fill in the missing numbers:

1, 2, _____ , 4, 5, _____ , 7, 8, _____ , 10, 11, _____ ,

13, 14, _____ , 16, 17, _____ , 19, 20, _____ , 22, 23,

_____ , 25, 26, _____ , 28, 29, _____

Mental Math 11

1. $10 + 80 =$ _____

2. $40 + 20 =$ _____

3. $60 + 20 =$ _____

4. $70 + 10 =$ _____

5. $80 + 20 =$ _____

6. $120 + 20 =$ _____

7. $540 + 30 =$ _____

8. $260 + 20 =$ _____

9. $320 + 50 =$ _____

10. $50 + 60 =$ _____

11. $70 + 70 =$ _____

12. $80 + 40 =$ _____

13. $60 + 60 =$ _____

14. $70 + 90 =$ _____

15. $90 + 50 =$ _____

16. $80 + 50 =$ _____

17. $60 + 70 =$ _____

18. $70 + 80 =$ _____

19. $80 + 30 =$ _____

20. $50 + 90 =$ _____

21. $70 + 40 =$ _____

22. $60 + 90 =$ _____

23. $60 + 50 =$ _____

24. $80 + 60 =$ _____

25. $60 + 70 =$ _____

26. $70 + 50 =$ _____

27. $50 + 80 =$ _____

28. $60 + 80 =$ _____

29. $70 + 60 =$ _____

30. $50 + 70 =$ _____

Mental Math 12

1. $430 + 2 =$ _____

2. $232 + 2 =$ _____

3. $764 + 2 =$ _____

4. $976 + 2 =$ _____

5. $188 + 2 =$ _____

6. $309 + 2 =$ _____

7. $404 + 9 =$ _____

8. $768 + 2 =$ _____

9. $918 + 2 =$ _____

10. $185 + 6 =$ _____

11. $487 + 7 =$ _____

12. $528 + 4 =$ _____

13. $876 + 6 =$ _____

14. $727 + 9 =$ _____

15. $269 + 5 =$ _____

16. $618 + 5 =$ _____

17. $526 + 7 =$ _____

18. $857 + 8 =$ _____

19. $148 + 2 =$ _____

20. $493 + 4 =$ _____

21. $307 + 4 =$ _____

22. $216 + 9 =$ _____

23. $626 + 3 =$ _____

24. $538 + 6 =$ _____

25. $876 + 7 =$ _____

26. $207 + 3 =$ _____

27. $315 + 8 =$ _____

28. $547 + 8 =$ _____

29. $947 + 6 =$ _____

30. $105 + 7 =$ _____

Mental Math 13

1. $80 - 20 =$ _____

2. $180 - 20 =$ _____

3. $110 - 20 =$ _____

4. $90 - 40 =$ _____

5. $190 - 40 =$ _____

6. $110 - 40 =$ _____

7. $100 - 20 =$ _____

8. $200 - 20 =$ _____

9. $100 - 70 =$ _____

10. $400 - 70 =$ _____

11. $110 - 60 =$ _____

12. $120 - 50 =$ _____

13. $110 - 90 =$ _____

14. $120 - 80 =$ _____

15. $130 - 50 =$ _____

16. $120 - 60 =$ _____

17. $120 - 70 =$ _____

18. $110 - 80 =$ _____

19. $200 - 60 =$ _____

20. $130 - 70 =$ _____

21. $120 - 40 =$ _____

22. $110 - 50 =$ _____

23. $130 - 60 =$ _____

24. $120 - 30 =$ _____

25. $130 - 80 =$ _____

26. $120 - 90 =$ _____

27. $130 - 40 =$ _____

28. $110 - 20 =$ _____

29. $130 - 90 =$ _____

30. $110 - 30 =$ _____

Mental Math 14

1. $100 - 30 =$ _____

2. $100 - 90 =$ _____

3. $100 - 50 =$ _____

4. $100 - 70 =$ _____

5. $160 - 70 =$ _____

6. $140 - 90 =$ _____

7. $190 - 70 =$ _____

8. $140 - 90 =$ _____

9. $140 - 30 =$ _____

10. $160 - 80 =$ _____

11. $170 - 90 =$ _____

12. $130 - 30 =$ _____

13. $130 - 70 =$ _____

14. $140 - 50 =$ _____

15. $150 - 90 =$ _____

16. $190 - 70 =$ _____

17. $140 - 60 =$ _____

18. $150 - 60 =$ _____

19. $120 - 90 =$ _____

20. $160 - 20 =$ _____

21. $140 - 80 =$ _____

22. $130 - 90 =$ _____

23. $150 - 70 =$ _____

24. $180 - 50 =$ _____

25. $170 - 30 =$ _____

26. $120 - 80 =$ _____

Fill in the missing numbers:

21, _____ , 19, _____ , 17, _____ , 15, _____ , 13, _____

11, _____ , 9, _____ , 7, _____ , 5, _____ , 3, _____

Mental Math 15

1. $160 - 90 =$ _____

2. $190 + 50 =$ _____

3. $60 + 50 =$ _____

4. $100 - 80 =$ _____

5. $200 - 50 =$ _____

6. $170 - 30 =$ _____

7. $50 + 90 =$ _____

8. $160 - 40 =$ _____

9. $20 + 90 =$ _____

10. $120 - 60 =$ _____

11. $160 - 80 =$ _____

12. $50 + 50 =$ _____

13. $70 + 80 =$ _____

14. $80 - 30 =$ _____

15. $150 - 70 =$ _____

16. $80 + 80 =$ _____

17. $60 + 60 =$ _____

18. $110 - 20 =$ _____

19. $190 - 60 =$ _____

20. $40 + 60 =$ _____

21. $80 + 90 =$ _____

22. $70 + 70 =$ _____

23. $110 - 30 =$ _____

24. $30 + 80 =$ _____

Fill in the missing numbers:

32, 31, _____ , 29, 28, _____ , 26, 25, _____ , 23, 22,

_____ , 20, 19, _____ , 17, 16, _____ , 14, 13, _____ , 11,

10, _____ , 8, 7, _____ , 5, 4, _____ , 2, 1

Mental Math 16

1. $930 - 3 =$ _____

2. $627 - 3 =$ _____

3. $424 - 2 =$ _____

4. $121 - 3 =$ _____

5. $818 - 3 =$ _____

6. $719 - 3 =$ _____

7. $603 - 5 =$ _____

8. $453 - 8 =$ _____

9. $243 - 6 =$ _____

10. $193 - 4 =$ _____

11. $204 - 7 =$ _____

12. $416 - 8 =$ _____

13. $657 - 9 =$ _____

14. $343 - 8 =$ _____

15. $713 - 7 =$ _____

16. $714 - 9 =$ _____

17. $896 - 2 =$ _____

18. $514 - 5 =$ _____

19. $385 - 9 =$ _____

20. $219 - 5 =$ _____

21. $974 - 6 =$ _____

22. $625 - 6 =$ _____

23. $562 - 9 =$ _____

24. $306 - 9 =$ _____

25. $934 - 8 =$ _____

26. $713 - 9 =$ _____

27. $875 - 7 =$ _____

28. $968 - 9 =$ _____

29. $507 - 4 =$ _____

30. $432 - 8 =$ _____

Mental Math 17

1. $140 - 9 = $ _____
2. $549 + 9 = $ _____
3. $686 + 5 = $ _____
4. $850 - 8 = $ _____
5. $246 + 5 = $ _____
6. $497 - 8 = $ _____
7. $334 + 9 = $ _____
8. $780 - 4 = $ _____
9. $632 + 9 = $ _____
10. $170 - 1 = $ _____
11. $246 - 8 = $ _____
12. $565 + 5 = $ _____
13. $635 + 9 = $ _____
14. $740 - 9 = $ _____
15. $1,000 - 8 = $ _____
16. $357 + 8 = $ _____
17. $268 - 3 = $ _____
18. $430 - 7 = $ _____
19. $788 + 8 = $ _____
20. $176 + 6 = $ _____
21. $960 - 2 = $ _____
22. $590 - 6 = $ _____
23. $664 + 6 = $ _____
24. $928 + 9 = $ _____
25. $837 + 7 = $ _____
26. $350 - 3 = $ _____
27. $483 + 8 = $ _____
28. $890 - 6 = $ _____
29. $857 + 8 = $ _____
30. $188 + 8 = $ _____

Mental Math 18

1. $4 + 7 - 2 + 1 =$ _____

2. $8 - 4 + 2 + 9 =$ _____

3. $9 + 8 - 6 - 2 =$ _____

4. $9 - 4 - 5 + 9 =$ _____

5. $8 + 7 + 2 - 9 - 2 =$ _____

6. $2 + 2 + 2 + 2 - 8 =$ _____

7. $1 + 7 + 5 - 4 + 3 =$ _____

8. $3 + 3 + 3 - 6 + 3 =$ _____

9. $9 - 7 + 3 - 1 + 8 - 5 =$ _____

10. $6 + 8 - 2 + 4 - 7 + 3 =$ _____

11. $2 + 2 + 2 + 2 + 2 + 2 =$ _____

12. $3 + 3 + 3 + 3 + 3 + 3 =$ _____

13. $4 + 9 - 2 + 8 - 3 - 7 + 4 =$ _____

14. $1 + 2 + 3 + 4 + 5 - 8 - 7 =$ _____

Finish the pattern:

2, 4, 6, 8, _____ , _____ , _____ , _____ , _____

Mental Math 19

1. $40 + 70 - 20 + 10 =$ _____

2. $80 + 90 - 40 + 20 =$ _____

3. $90 - 20 + 80 - 60 =$ _____

4. $90 - 40 - 50 + 80 =$ _____

5. $80 + 70 + 20 - 80 - 20 =$ _____

6. $20 + 20 + 20 + 20 - 50 =$ _____

7. $10 + 70 + 60 - 40 + 30 =$ _____

8. $30 + 30 + 30 - 50 + 20 =$ _____

9. $90 - 20 - 30 - 10 + 80 - 50 =$ _____

10. $60 + 80 - 30 + 40 - 70 + 50 =$ _____

11. $20 + 20 + 20 + 20 + 20 + 20 + 20 =$ _____

12. $30 + 30 + 30 + 30 + 30 + 30 + 30 =$ _____

13. $40 + 90 + 20 - 80 - 30 - 70 + 40 =$ _____

14. $10 + 20 + 30 + 40 + 50 + 60 + 70 =$ _____

Finish the pattern:

10, 12, 14, _____ , _____ , _____ , _____ , _____

Mental Math 20

1. $23 + 10 - 1 + 4 =$ _____

2. $48 - 4 + 2 - 9 =$ _____

3. $69 + 8 - 6 - 20 =$ _____

4. $92 - 4 - 50 + 9 =$ _____

5. $8 + 27 + 2 - 9 - 20 =$ _____

6. $20 + 20 + 22 + 2 - 8 =$ _____

7. $11 + 7 + 50 - 40 + 3 =$ _____

8. $30 + 30 + 30 - 6 - 3 =$ _____

9. $95 - 7 + 30 - 10 + 8 - 5 =$ _____

10. $6 + 48 - 2 + 40 - 7 + 30 =$ _____

11. $72 + 20 - 30 + 4 + 2 + 2 =$ _____

12. $30 + 3 + 3 + 3 + 3 + 3 =$ _____

13. $14 + 9 - 2 + 20 - 30 - 7 + 4 =$ _____

14. $10 + 20 + 30 + 40 - 50 - 8 - 7 =$ _____

Finish the pattern:

3, 6, 9, _____ , _____ , _____ , _____ , _____

Mental Math 21

1. $917 + 20 =$ _____

2. $643 + 50 =$ _____

3. $235 - 20 =$ _____

4. $462 + 30 =$ _____

5. $799 - 20 =$ _____

6. $381 + 40 =$ _____

7. $563 - 50 =$ _____

8. $474 - 30 =$ _____

9. $617 + 50 =$ _____

10. $268 - 20 =$ _____

11. $821 + 40 =$ _____

12. $984 - 70 =$ _____

13. $526 + 60 =$ _____

14. $747 - 20 =$ _____

15. $136 + 50 =$ _____

16. $341 + 40 =$ _____

17. $150 - 20 =$ _____

18. $248 + 30 =$ _____

19. $564 + 10 =$ _____

20. $391 - 30 =$ _____

21. $115 + 70 =$ _____

22. $462 - 30 =$ _____

23. $986 - 20 =$ _____

24. $779 - 60 =$ _____

25. $355 + 20 =$ _____

26. $483 - 40 =$ _____

27. $622 + 70 =$ _____

28. $898 - 70 =$ _____

Finish the pattern:

3, 6, 9, _____ , _____ , _____ , _____ , _____ , _____ , _____

Mental Math 22

1. $461 + 300 =$ _____

2. $394 - 50 =$ _____

3. $490 + 2 =$ _____

4. $978 - 100 =$ _____

5. $342 - 4 =$ _____

6. $5 + 378 =$ _____

7. $200 + 459 =$ _____

8. $821 - 9 =$ _____

9. $891 - 20 =$ _____

10. $30 + 29 =$ _____

11. $8 + 64 =$ _____

12. $458 - 4 =$ _____

13. $458 - 40 =$ _____

14. $458 - 400 =$ _____

15. $110 - 9 =$ _____

16. $110 - 90 =$ _____

17. $800 + 200 =$ _____

18. $705 - 400 =$ _____

19. $6 + 314 =$ _____

20. $60 + 314 =$ _____

21. $600 + 384 =$ _____

22. $745 - 40 =$ _____

23. $459 + 30 - 80 + 2 =$ _____

24. $700 - 2 - 5 - 8 + 10 =$ _____

25. $875 - 300 + 400 - 75 =$ _____

26. $3 + 4 + 40 + 20 + 400 =$ _____

Mental Math 23

X	1	2	3	4	5	6	7	8	9	10
1										
2										
3										
4										
5										
6										
7										
8										
9										
10										

Mental Math 24

x	5	10	2	1	8	9	3	7	4	6
1										
2										

x	3	6	1	9	5	4	7	10	8	2
2										
1										

x	1	4	5	2	7	3	8	9	6	1
1										
2										

Mental Math 25

1. $1 \times 1 = $ _____

2. $2 \times 6 = $ _____

3. $2 \times 8 = $ _____

4. $1 \times 5 = $ _____

5. $1 \times 9 = $ _____

6. $2 \times 2 = $ _____

7. $1 \times 8 = $ _____

8. $2 \times 9 = $ _____

9. $1 \times 6 = $ _____

10. $1 \times 10 = $ _____

11. $2 \times 2 = $ _____

12. $6 \times 1 = $ _____

13. $8 \times 2 = $ _____

14. $5 \times 1 = $ _____

15. $8 \times 2 = $ _____

16. $2 \times 4 = $ _____

17. $1 \times 2 = $ _____

18. $2 \times 7 = $ _____

19. $1 \times 3 = $ _____

20. $2 \times 10 = $ _____

21. $2 \times 3 = $ _____

22. $1 \times 4 = $ _____

23. $2 \times 2 = $ _____

24. $2 \times 5 = $ _____

25. $1 \times 7 = $ _____

26. $9 \times 2 = $ _____

27. $3 \times 2 = $ _____

28. $7 \times 2 = $ _____

29. $4 \times 2 = $ _____

30. $6 \times 2 = $ _____

Mental Math 26

X	1	2	3	4	5	6	7	8	9	10
1										
2										
3										
4										
5										
6										
7										
8										
9										
10										

Mental Math 27

X	5	10	2	1	8	9	3	7	4	6
1										
2										
3										

X	3	6	1	9	5	4	7	10	8	2
2										
1										
3										

X	1	4	5	2	7	3	8	9	6	1
1										
3										
2										

Mental Math 28

1. $3 \times 1 =$ _____

2. $2 \times 5 =$ _____

3. $2 \times 6 =$ _____

4. $2 \times 10 =$ _____

5. $3 \times 5 =$ _____

6. $2 \times 4 =$ _____

7. $3 \times 8 =$ _____

8. $3 \times 10 =$ _____

9. $2 \times 8 =$ _____

10. $3 \times 7 =$ _____

11. $7 \times 2 =$ _____

12. $5 \times 3 =$ _____

13. $10 \times 3 =$ _____

14. $7 \times 3 =$ _____

15. $9 \times 3 =$ _____

16. $2 \times 3 =$ _____

17. $3 \times 2 =$ _____

18. $3 \times 9 =$ _____

19. $3 \times 4 =$ _____

20. $9 \times 3 =$ _____

21. $3 \times 3 =$ _____

22. $2 \times 2 =$ _____

23. $2 \times 9 =$ _____

24. $2 \times 7 =$ _____

25. $3 \times 6 =$ _____

26. $8 \times 2 =$ _____

27. $8 \times 3 =$ _____

28. $6 \times 3 =$ _____

29. $9 \times 2 =$ _____

30. $4 \times 3 =$ _____

Mental Math 29

1. $16 \div 2 =$ _____

2. $1 \div 1 =$ _____

3. $4 \div 1 =$ _____

4. $18 \div 2 =$ _____

5. $2 \div 1 =$ _____

6. $6 \div 2 =$ _____

7. $7 \div 1 =$ _____

8. $4 \div 2 =$ _____

9. $8 \div 2 =$ _____

10. $6 \div 1 =$ _____

11. $6 \div 2 =$ _____

12. $14 \div 2 =$ _____

13. $12 \div 2 =$ _____

14. $4 \div 2 =$ _____

15. $36 \div 1 =$ _____

16. $10 \div 1 =$ _____

17. $20 \div 2 =$ _____

18. $14 \div 2 =$ _____

19. $5 \div 1 =$ _____

20. $12 \div 2 =$ _____

21. $3 \div 1 =$ _____

22. $9 \div 1 =$ _____

23. $10 \div 2 =$ _____

24. $8 \div 1 =$ _____

25. $2 \div 2 =$ _____

26. $10 \div 2 =$ _____

27. $16 \div 2 =$ _____

28. $8 \div 2 =$ _____

29. $18 \div 2 =$ _____

30. $458 \div 1 =$ _____

Mental Math 30

1. $27 \div 3 =$ _____
2. $2 \div 2 =$ _____
3. $15 \div 3 =$ _____
4. $8 \div 2 =$ _____
5. $20 \div 2 =$ _____
6. $6 \div 3 =$ _____
7. $14 \div 2 =$ _____
8. $16 \div 2 =$ _____
9. $21 \div 3 =$ _____
10. $14 \div 2 =$ _____
11. $6 \div 3 =$ _____
12. $24 \div 3 =$ _____
13. $15 \div 3 =$ _____
14. $27 \div 3 =$ _____
15. $30 \div 3 =$ _____
16. $9 \div 3 =$ _____
17. $6 \div 2 =$ _____
18. $30 \div 3 =$ _____
19. $3 \div 3 =$ _____
20. $24 \div 3 =$ _____
21. $4 \div 2 =$ _____
22. $12 \div 3 =$ _____
23. $10 \div 2 =$ _____
24. $18 \div 3 =$ _____
25. $12 \div 2 =$ _____
26. $21 \div 3 =$ _____
27. $9 \div 3 =$ _____
28. $3 \div 3 =$ _____
29. $18 \div 3 =$ _____
30. $12 \div 3 =$ _____

Mental Math 31

1. $8 \div 1 = \underline{\hspace{2cm}}$

2. $30 \div 3 = \underline{\hspace{2cm}}$

3. $4 \times 2 = \underline{\hspace{2cm}}$

4. $10 \times 3 = \underline{\hspace{2cm}}$

5. $21 \div 3 = \underline{\hspace{2cm}}$

6. $27 \div 3 = \underline{\hspace{2cm}}$

7. $6 \times 3 = \underline{\hspace{2cm}}$

8. $2 \times 9 = \underline{\hspace{2cm}}$

9. $12 \div 2 = \underline{\hspace{2cm}}$

10. $3 \times 8 = \underline{\hspace{2cm}}$

11. $3 \times 7 = \underline{\hspace{2cm}}$

12. $15 \div 3 = \underline{\hspace{2cm}}$

13. $7 \times 2 = \underline{\hspace{2cm}}$

14. $9 \times 1 = \underline{\hspace{2cm}}$

15. $2 \times 6 = \underline{\hspace{2cm}}$

16. $3 \times 2 = \underline{\hspace{2cm}}$

17. $10 \times 2 = \underline{\hspace{2cm}}$

18. $1 \times 3 = \underline{\hspace{2cm}}$

19. $3 \div 3 = \underline{\hspace{2cm}}$

20. $5 \times 3 = \underline{\hspace{2cm}}$

21. $27 \div 3 = \underline{\hspace{2cm}}$

22. $7 \times 3 = \underline{\hspace{2cm}}$

23. $6 \div 3 = \underline{\hspace{2cm}}$

24. $2 \times 3 = \underline{\hspace{2cm}}$

25. $20 \div 2 = \underline{\hspace{2cm}}$

26. $8 \div 2 = \underline{\hspace{2cm}}$

27. $18 \div 3 = \underline{\hspace{2cm}}$

28. $6 \div 2 = \underline{\hspace{2cm}}$

29. $18 \div 2 = \underline{\hspace{2cm}}$

30. $6 \times 2 = \underline{\hspace{2cm}}$

Mental Math 32

1. $8 \times 2 =$ _____

2. $9 \times 3 =$ _____

3. $14 \div 2 =$ _____

4. $12 \div 3 =$ _____

5. $8 \times 3 =$ _____

6. $3 \times 7 =$ _____

7. $21 \div 3 =$ _____

8. $9 \times 2 =$ _____

9. $4 \div 2 =$ _____

10. $2 \times 2 =$ _____

11. $9 \times 3 =$ _____

12. $16 \div 2 =$ _____

13. $2 \times 7 =$ _____

14. $5 \times 2 =$ _____

15. $1 \times 324 =$ _____

16. $3 \times 3 =$ _____

17. $16 \div 2 =$ _____

18. $9 \div 3 =$ _____

19. $24 \div 3 =$ _____

20. $2 \times 8 =$ _____

21. $18 \div 2 =$ _____

22. $12 \div 3 =$ _____

23. $18 \div 3 =$ _____

24. $6 \div 1 =$ _____

25. $14 \div 2 =$ _____

26. $4 \times 3 =$ _____

27. $3 \times 9 =$ _____

28. $2 \div 2 =$ _____

29. $1 \times 2 =$ _____

30. $84 \div 1 =$ _____

Multiplication by 2 or 3 Game Board

21	16	9	4	12	18
24	2	14	27	30	15
20	16	18	3	6	2
4	8	6	12	12	24
10	18	21	18	10	6
12	9	27	20	15	30
6	3	8	27	14	2

Division by 2 or 3 Game Board

3	8	2	4	6	☆
4	9	1	5	7	3
7	5	10	8	6	10
9	8	2	1	10	3
4	6	1	5	6	7
2	10	5	8	7	2
☆	8	9	3	4	1

Multiplication and Division by 2 or 3 Game Board

3	8	4	18	6	☆
24	9	6	21	7	3
7	30	10	15	8	2
12	8	2	1	10	12
4	6	10	5	9	14
30	3	5	16	6	2
☆	8	18	27	4	1